X2 Patrol

Contents

Acknowledgements

John Olivey's story is published courtesy of his eldest son, Peter John 'P. J.' Olivey, who also provided important background detail, as did John Olivey's grandson, Dick Hayter. Craig Gomm and Patricia Hutchings acquired from the National Archives of Zimbabwe John Olivey's 'personal narrative' as recorded by Major Cecil W. Mercer; Tim Broderick provided material relating to his father, 'Brick' Broderick (LRDG); Angela Lench and David Murphy shared information about their father, 'Spud' Murphy; Daniel Kirmatzis made available the prisoner of war log of Bill Taylor (4 Buffs), Nikolai Debono digitised hundreds of pages of documents at The National Archives in the UK, and Ian Chard and Wes Richards each selflessly shared a wealth of their own research material. Thank you to everyone and to Jeff Sammut for his Italian to English translations, and, for the images, Michael Xenikakis, Andreas Galanos, Vassilis Mentogiannis, Mark Millar, Brendan O'Carroll, Jonathan Pittaway, and Rachel Roberts at Lancaster City Museum. For information about New Zealanders in the LRDG, I thank the New Zealand Defence Force and Auckland War Memorial Museum. I also wish to acknowledge the past help of those who served on both sides in the Aegean during the Second World War and who are no longer with us, notably Ron Hill, Jim Patch and John Kevan (all LRDG) and Gustav Wehrs (Wehrmacht). My appreciation, too, to Jessica Cuthbert-Smith for her faultless copyediting, and to Steve Williamson for typesetting and proofreading. And a heartfelt *vielen Dank* to my partner Bettina Selke for her tireless support, help and enthusiasm during what has been a most enjoyable writing experience.

Introduction

by Anthony Rogers

During the Second World War, unorthodox military formations, 'Special Forces' in today's parlance, featured in both the Allied and Axis orders of battle (ORBATs). Britain's prime minister, Winston Churchill, was a keen advocate of irregular warfare and openly encouraged and supported the concept. One of the first such units of the British Army was the brainchild of an accomplished desert explorer and geologist, Brigadier Ralph A. Bagnold. Established in July 1940 mainly with New Zealanders, No. 1 Long Range Patrol Unit would, by the end of the year, be restructured and renamed the Long Range Desert Group (LRDG). This highly effective mobile reconnaissance force operated behind enemy lines, sometimes in conjunction with another wartime addition to the British Army's ORBAT, the Special Air Service (SAS).

Extraordinary organisations attract extraordinary individuals. One such man was John Richard Olivey. He was born on 11 December 1905 in Poole in the county of Dorset, England. Educated at Maidenhead and King's School, Ely, he went on to read medicine at Sidney Sussex College, Cambridge. It seemed he would follow in his father's footsteps by becoming a doctor, but the young Olivey then took a very different course, and in April 1925, age 19, left England for South Africa. Initially, he spent time in the Cape Border area, before acquiring experience as a sheep farmer in the Orange Free State and eventually heading north to Rhodesia (present-day Zimbabwe). At Trelawney, north-west of Salisbury (now, Harare), he learned how to grow tobacco. Olivey spent two years in Africa, and then returned to England. He did not stay long. By February 1928, he was back in Rhodesia.

Having decided that sheep ranching offered better prospects than did growing and selling tobacco, Olivey purchased Sawerombi, a farm in the Melsetter district (today, Chimanimani). Life was often tough for even the hardiest of settlers. At Melsetter, a mountainous region bordering Mozambique, the climate, rugged terrain, wildlife and more could be challenging. Olivey persevered, and in time, would prosper. He married Thelma Alexandra Siebert, a schoolteacher, and in November 1932 she gave birth to a daughter, Annabel. The marriage would end tragically and all too soon. In August 1937, Thelma Olivey became gravely ill. Three weeks later, she was dead. Thelma's sister Nova and her husband Russel Barnes were entrusted with raising Annabel. Olivey would not remarry until several years later, by which time, the world was at war.

In October 1939, at the age of nearly 34, John Olivey enlisted in His Majesty's armed forces. Initially, he served as a corporal in 1st Battalion The Sherwood Foresters (Nottingham and Derbyshire Regiment) and in April 1940 boarded the troopship *Karanja* for passage to Egypt. From there he continued to Cyprus. Before long, Olivey had applied for a commission, returning to the battalion some four months later as a junior officer. He joined the LRDG in 1941. Before the year was over, he was awarded the Military Cross (MC). The citation provides a glimpse into the modus operandi of the LRDG at this time and of Olivey's seemingly fearless nature:

'2/Lt. J. R. Olivey's Patrol was ordered to attack enemy transport on the BARCE – DERNA road some 150 miles behind the enemy lines. During the night of 29/11/41, having made a personal reconnaissance on foot, he led his Patrol in bright moonlight along the road and attacked at point blank range all vehicles which were encountered.

'His Patrol inflicted considerable damage on an Eastbound convoy of 6 heavy lorries with trailers, killing the crews and wrecking the lorries. He then organised an ambush which resulted in the destruction of a further four vehicles with their crews. The success of the operation was largely due to 2/Lt. Olivey's careful planning and cool leadership.'

With the imminent defeat of the *Deutsches Afrikakorps* in Tunisia, on 1 April 1943 a General Headquarters directive detailed what was expected of the LRDG in future operations. The unit War Diary records:

'This Directive, in brief, required the Unit to be able to operate by Jeep or on foot in mountainous country with the object of liaison with Patriot forces. It was necessary therefore to readjust our ideas completely and to arrange a comprehensive training programme. The 2 i/c. [second-in-command], Major EASONSMITH went to SYRIA to find a suitable training ground, and was fortunate in being able to arrange for the Unit to take over the CEDARS HOTEL in the LEBANON MOUNTAINS, which hitherto [had] been used by the ME [Middle East] Ski School. This building is situated in perfect training country at 6300 feet, with mountains up to 10.000 feet in the close proximity.'

The LRDG was to spend the next few months retraining in unfamiliar terrain. For Olivey, by this time second-in-command of B Squadron, this included learning to ski. There were also arduous load carries and rock climbing, and even practical lessons in handling pack mules. Parachute training had just started, when it was brought to an abrupt end by the Italian armistice in September 1943.

Olivey had excelled in North Africa. He would continue to do so in the Dodecanese in autumn 1943, by which time the LRDG consisted of a Headquarters and two squadrons. A Squadron was manned primarily by New Zealanders, and B Squadron by British and Rhodesians; each squadron was about 300 strong. The familiar image of bearded warriors criss-crossing the desert in well-armed Chevrolets was over, the LRDG patrol vehicles having been handed in and largely replaced by ex-SAS jeeps. Furthermore, when the LRDG embarked for passage to the Aegean, they did so without any transport. During their next phase of operations, the LRDG were to take on a static role, manning island outposts, and as would happen at Levitha and Leros, sometimes serving as infantry. (LRDG Captain Dudley C. Folland later arranged for four jeeps to be delivered to Leros, only for them to be routinely commandeered by Brigade Headquarters.)

By the end of November 1943, after more than two months of air, sea and land operations, German forces had taken control of practically all the Dodecanese. Thousands of Italians and mainly British forces were taken prisoner, among them, Captain John Olivey.

When he was in Rhodesia on home leave in November 1942, Olivey had married Mary Madge (aka Mickey) née Tollner, a non-commissioned officer in the South African Corps of Signals. It was while he was in hiding in Greece after having escaped German captivity that Olivey wrote for Mickey what he would describe as a letter. This, a very detailed memoir relating his experiences in the Aegean and in Athens, he titled *Fee, Fie, Foe, Fum.*

In 1963, the 'letter' was copy typed by Rosemary Smuts, private secretary of T. C. (Tommy) Haddon. At some point, another typescript was produced, a copy of which was provided by Haddon to his former commanding officer in the LRDG, David L. Lloyd Owen.

This would eventually end up amongst Lloyd Owen's papers at the Imperial War Museum in London, where I discovered it while researching my book about the 1943 war in the Aegean, *Churchill's Folly*. It differs from that produced by Ms Smuts only in its improved punctuation and very occasional clarification of otherwise confusing phrasing. Both documents are the basis for this book (the handwritten original has been lost).

Olivey had attached to the typescript produced by Ms Smuts a cover note, remarking somewhat prophetically, 'the story could be continued some day with my escape to Turkey – the journey to Cairo with Fraulein Kapp (operation Cicero).'

I like to think that John Olivey would have approved of what follows. His narrative is reproduced with the omission of only a few passages that might be deemed irrelevant, and the repositioning of several paragraphs that were better suited chronologically for the prologue. I have taken Haddon's improvements further, for example, by inserting a missing part of speech and correcting obvious typographical errors. Olivey's sometimes unusual syntax remains largely unchanged, however.

I have indicated with [---] where words are missing, due to their being illegible in the original handwritten manuscript (or, in at least two instances, probably because they were mild expletives).

Neither Rosemary Smuts nor Tommy Haddon (who had joined the LRDG after the conclusion of 1943 Aegean operations) would have been familiar with many of the people and places Olivey wrote about. This may partly explain why so many names are missing from the typescripts. It is also very likely that Olivey chose not to include them for security reasons, lest he be recaptured with the 'letter' in his possession. Whatever the reason, placenames and the identities of more than forty people were concealed. Wherever possible, I have rectified this, referring to locations and people by their true names. Exceptions include some of the Greek people whom Olivey encountered in and around Athens. Typical is a woman loathed by Olivey and referred to as Mad. It is unclear if this is a diminutive of her real name, or perhaps, given Olivey's special brand of humour, a facetious reference to her perceived state of mind.

In order to clarify and expand on events, I have drawn on primary sources to provide a running commentary, and also include supplementary material from a recording made in summer 1944 by Major Cecil W. Mercer (aka Dornford Yates), I hope without interrupting the flow of John Olivey's own narrative.

FEE FIE FOE FUM,
I SMELL THE BLOOD OF A GERMAN HUN,
WHETHER HE BE ALIVE OR HE BE DEAD,
I'LL GRIND HIS BONES TO MAKE MY BREAD.

John Olivey
– adaptation of a childhood rhyme

Prologue

At the age of six or seven, I used to delight in getting out of bed after my governess had put me to bed and creeping downstairs and hiding behind the big thick curtains which used to hang in the alcoves of our box windows and staying there while my parents had dinner. I always chose nights when I knew they were expecting visitors. I then used to have a good listening post for their conversations. In these days, before the Great War, conversation used to often be about the Germans and of possible invasion, until I, as a child, became convinced that the Germans were some dreadful bogie man who threatened our lives. There was an oldish clergyman who often used to be present and he was quite convinced, I remember, that the Germans would invade. Our house was quite close to the main street, a big old-fashioned house with a garden in front. There were often noises in the street which used to frighten me as a child, when alone upstairs. One night, as I was hiding behind the curtain, there was a tremendous noise in the street. I rather think now they were celebrating Guy Fawkes, or the like, but in any case, one of the wits at dinner turned to the other and said to him, "Ah, there are your Germans arrived at last!" It was enough for me. I let out a tremendous bellow and collapsed. Everyone was surprised. I suppose the governess got choked off, poor girl, it was not her fault. Anyway, special precautions were taken to see I was in bed at dinner time except by organised arrangement, when my sister would be allowed down as well. I suffered dreadfully for years afterwards with Germans chasing me, though I had no idea who the Germans were. Until war broke out in 1914 – we were then staying at the seaside and we used to watch the soldiers go off by train and lived in fear that my father, who was a doctor, would go off with the next train. I had a second great fright when, in a seaside lane one day, some cavalry

> came galloping down. I again thought it was the Germans and ran to my mother. She, wise woman, said, "Oh! But you wouldn't run away from the Germans would you? And in any case, these are our brave soldiers going to fight them."
>
> From that day on, I resolved I would never run away again. I went through my early school days in a sort of perpetual state of steeling myself to fight Germans. I was certainly not born without nerves and it cost me more than I like to think of those days in courage and worry, until I used to make myself quite ill with childish results which no one could ever understand and I also learnt nothing, which is not surprising when it is considered how I was fighting the Great War at the same time.

John Olivey's reminiscences provide a glimpse into the over-active imagination of a child raised in upper-middle-class England in the early twentieth century. Recalling his schooldays, Olivey also described how, during morning prayers, the headmaster would read through the newspaper daily casualty list. Recognising the name of a former pupil, the headmaster would pause, before addressing his audience with an appropriate comment. Such occasions were to make a lasting impression on young Olivey. He was nearly 13 years of age when the First World War came to an end.

> When the Armistice (1918) was declared, I was quite ready. Why, I don't know, but I had brought my bugle to school that day. We were on drill parade at 11 o'clock when the sirens sounded and all the ships started hooting. Our sergeant major drill instructor of Boer War days asked what it was all about. I replied that peace had been signed. How I knew, I can't say, but I certainly did before the masters or any of the others. I then produced my bugle and blew and blew and blew. I felt I had beaten the Germans on my own. It had cost me dearly, however.
>
> When war seemed likely in 1932, I joined the territorials and worked my way with a rifle up to commissioned rank. When war broke out in 1939, I immediately hoped to be called up. As it was the policy of our government to leave all farmers on the land, I

wasn't. I rebelled and I fear was rather rude all round to ministers and government officials, telling any sort of lie, but go I would. I was eventually called in October and have since been able to satisfy my boyish hopes and aims.

CHAPTER 1

Improvise and Dare

The North African campaign had ended with the surrender of the *Afrikakorps* in Tunisia in May 1943. The Allied invasion of Sicily, codename 'Husky', commenced two months later on 10 July. Faced with an imminent invasion of the mainland, the Fascist Grand Council in Italy passed a vote of no confidence in their leader, Benito Mussolini. He was ousted on 25 July and Maresciallo Pietro Badoglio became Italy's new prime minister.

There followed secret negotiations with the United States and Britain, culminating in an armistice that was agreed on 3 September 1943 and announced five days later. For Germany's Führer, Adolf Hitler, this only increased the risk to his nation's interests in the eastern Mediterranean. The German war effort was partly reliant on natural resources imported from the region. Greece was a valuable source of ore, including chrome (used in armoured steel production) and bauxite (from which aluminium was extracted). There was also the Allied threat to Romania and the Ploesti oilfields to consider. Hitler had anticipated Italy's volte-face, however, and responded with countermeasures under the codename 'Achse' (Axis). His forces soon seized control from the Italians in Crete, but were slower in reacting to the situation elsewhere.

The British, too, were determined to establish a presence in the region, focusing primarily on the Dodecanese in the eastern Aegean. First, it was deemed necessary to secure Rhodes, with its all-important airfields. This would jeopardise the German positions in Crete and provide a base for effective action in the Aegean. Italian cooperation was essential to British plans.

The task of securing Rhodes was allocated to 234 Infantry Brigade recently arrived in the Middle East from Malta. A military mission was to precede the expedition, while the Special Boat Squadron (SBS) spearheaded the occupation of other islands, including Kastellorizo, Kos and Samos. Winston Churchill was a keen advocate of the plan, which was approved by him on 9 September: 'Good. This is a time to play high. Improvise and dare.'

On 9 September 1943, a three-man team headed by the SBS commanding officer Major Lord George P. J. R. Jellicoe parachuted in to Rhodes to establish contact with the Italian Governor, Ammiraglio Inigo Campioni. Two days later, on 11 September, the German *Sturmdivision Rhodos*, numbering approximately 7,500 men, seized control of the island, taking prisoner 35,000–40,000 Italians, thus ending British hopes of an assisted take-over.

Without Rhodes, there was little or no prospect of continuing operations in the Aegean. This was clearly understood by the Commander-in-Chief, Middle East and the British Chiefs of Staff and Allied Headquarters. Nonetheless, and against the advice of his American allies, Churchill persevered. Operations were to continue, but on a reduced scale.

German resources in the Aegean had been stretched by their deployments in Rhodes and Crete. It seemed possible, therefore, that by acting quickly, British forces might yet obtain control elsewhere, thereby detracting from recent enemy successes, while enhancing British prestige throughout the Middle East and at the same time providing a diversion for Allied operations in Italy. Even with the limited means available, the occupation of Kos, Leros and Samos could still succeed.

The number of German aircraft in the region did not yet represent a serious threat. With British fighters based at Kos, the only unoccupied island with a sizeable airfield, there was little possibility of major German seaborne or airborne operations. It was thought that with Italian cooperation, British forces might maintain themselves in Kos and Leros until an attack could be launched on Rhodes from the Middle East.

During the night of 12/13 September, a small party of SBS was taken by motor launch to Kos. From there, Major Jellicoe proceeded to Leros. Major David Lloyd Owen, commanding B Squadron of the LRDG, landed at Leros with Y Patrol early in the morning of 15 September. Meanwhile, A Company of 11th Battalion The Parachute Regiment were dropped on Kos, to be followed a day later by an advance party of 1st Battalion The Durham Light Infantry. SBS under Major David G. C. Sutherland proceeded to Samos. On the 17th, A and B Companies of 2nd Battalion The Royal Irish Fusiliers (Faughs) together with headquarters personnel and stores reached Leros on board the British destroyers *Hurworth* and *Croome*.

Reinforcements, including B Company of 2nd Battalion The Queen's Own Royal West Kent Regiment, arrived at Kastellorizo. The remainder of the Royal West Kents were deployed later in the month to garrison the island of Samos (a platoon subsequently occupied neighbouring Ikaria), while the LRDG went on to set up base at Kalymnos and sending patrols as far west as the Cyclades.

By 19 September, therefore, British forces had established a presence in the region. But so, too, had German forces, with troops occupying Thasos, Samothraki, Limnos, Lesbos, Chios, islands in the Sporades and the Cyclades, Kasos, Karpathos, Kythira and Antikythira as well as Crete and Rhodes.

Following the armistice, Italians were divided in their loyalties. Those who displayed a willingness to change sides ran a terrible risk. On 11 September, Hitler issued a fateful directive:

'By order of the Führer, all Italian units which have allowed their weapons to fall into the hands of the insurgents or even collaborated with the insurgents are, when captured, to be dealt with as follows:

'1. Officers are to be shot in accordance with martial law.

'2. Petty officers and men are to be transported directly to the east, if possible avoiding transportation routes through the Reich, by Chief, Prisoners of War, General War Administration Bureau, Armed Forces High Command and placed at the disposal of Quartermaster General, Army General Staff for employment.'

Two days later, at Kefallonia in the Ionian Islands, Italian coastal batteries engaged two German landing craft, sinking one and damaging the other. It was the beginning of a battle that would result in the deaths of many of the 12,000 Italian officers and men on the island. In addition to those killed in battle, thousands were executed or perished en route to labour camps after their transport ships were lost to mines. Kefallonia was the worst massacre of pro-Badoglio Italians, but Italian officers would also be executed elsewhere, notably the islands of Kos and to a lesser degree, Leros, where the LRDG was very nearly destroyed as an effective unit.

Leros lies beyond Kalymnos towards the northern extremity of the Dodecanese. It is an island of irregular shape, some 9 miles (14.5 kilometres) in length and varying in width from approximately 0.8 miles (1.3 kilometres) to a little over 4 miles (6.4 kilometres), with nearby islets mainly in the north and south-east. Leros is predominantly rocky with deep valleys and rugged windswept hills, the highest of which is Mount Scumbarda (Point 334) in the south. The island has a much indented and fairly inhospitable coastline, with only a few sandy beaches mainly in the central region. The capital, Platanos (formerly Lero), is situated more or less centrally in a narrow coastal valley, overlooked to the north-east by a medieval castle (atop Point 189). Further east is Appetici (Point 180), and, to the south, Mount Meraviglia (Point 204). A road runs the length of the island, linking the town with Parteni in the north and the chief port of Lakki (previously Portolago) in the south. A notable feature of Leros in 1943 was its twenty-five heavy gun batteries, which were situated throughout the island.

The Italians on Leros enjoyed a comfortable existence, some even residing there with their families. Local Greeks led a more austere lifestyle and existed by farming small terraced plots on hillside slopes, as shepherds, goatherds and fishermen. In 1943, after more than twenty years of Italian rule, the two nationalities had learned to tolerate each other, and so far, Leros had escaped the fate of other disputed islands in the Mediterranean. This was soon to change.

CHAPTER 2

Phase 12

Friday, 10 September 1943. At Ramat David, Palestine, 110 officers and other ranks (ORs) of B Squadron of the LRDG had reached the final day of ground training, ready for their first parachute jump the next morning. Captain John Richard Olivey was looking forward to the experience.

> For some months now I have not felt in better health. The course has been a strenuous one and after our training in the mountains with the rock climbing, skiing, weight carrying and now our runs and gymnastics, I feel I could jump over the moon. That's how I feel, but in point of fact, it may be far simpler, for as David [Lloyd Owen] has put it, "any fool can jump out of an aeroplane!" But then, David is regular Army and is not jumping himself. Not that I don't want to jump, but as the instructor said, "when one is going up to jump, everyone makes silly jokes at which no one laughs and all are wondering why they volunteered for this branch of the Army."

Having drawn helmet and coveralls, John Olivey strolled back to his tent, where he was greeted by Major J. R. (Jake) Easonsmith, who handed him a signal. It was an order for everybody to be ready to move at two-hours' notice. Easonsmith left that evening to be briefed, leaving Olivey in charge of packing in preparation for the move.

The news quickly spread. Most, if not all, on the course regretted not being able to experience at least one parachute descent. Making the best of the situation, it was instead arranged to meet the parachute jump instructors that evening for a farewell drink in the Sergeants' Mess. Notwithstanding wartime rationing, there was more than enough alcohol. Beer was followed by gin, which was in turn followed by whisky.

Having applauded the sentimental songs, laughed at the usual dirty jokes, we ended with sticks of ten jumping off the bar. Everyone agreed the course knew its stuff. If only we could jump tomorrow. We have learnt to call each other 'chappies' and to get the 'grif' or 'gen'.

The next day brings a grim headache after all the mixtures. This is hardly surprising. One always is surprised, however. The Unit moves off early. Somehow, I manage to be the last to leave and in so doing, get two good breakfasts. I join the Unit in -Aren [sic] and find them installed in an old monastery. I carry my kit up two flights of stairs and sit down exhausted for a rest before drawing odds and ends to bring myself up to the establishment. There is very little I require as I have always managed to get things when others seem to have failed – a few rounds of revolver ammo, an odd mob strap and I am complete. The senior officers go to a conference and return at about midday. We are to move out of No. - Area to a camp up the road. I am given the special job of going back to Ramat David and collecting a Eureka set. These sets are for directing aircraft to a given spot and then signalling the moment a parachute will drop. It's their last set at Ramat David and I have to sign that our need is for operational purposes and that we will return the two we have for training as soon as possible. I sign all these things hoping they are true, seeing I have not been told why we need it or if it is possible to return the others. Everyone is very helpful at Ramat David and the set, complete with aerial, is soon on its way. I have also collected table tops and trestles, which are more precious than gold. My 15 cwt. and 2 x 3-tonners are loaded up and we proceed on our way after tea.

The camp was easy to find and is already occupied by another unit of our force. We dine in the Mess and bunk down in a tent. The ground is not level and my feet go to sleep sounder than most

> of my body. I rise with the sun, shave and with Stanley [Lieutenant Stanley N. Eastwood], go off for a bath. The water is rough and the beach rocky. A surf side throws me on the rocks and grazes my side and hips, but why worry? It was a good swim and breakfast goes down well. After breakfast, a grand sort out of kit takes place. I never can make up my mind what to take and what to leave and usually take far too much. This time I am limited, as I have to carry all I take. Three valises, a sleeping bag and set belt and equipment make my load. The rest of my kit goes in a kit bag and is to be returned to our quarters. Ah, yes! And with me goes my small attaché case with my precious photographs, my camera and writing gear.
>
> We are to move at 1600 hours and proceed to the assembly area. Everyone starts to speculate our possible destination and no one knows. My throat is sore but that will get right in time. We move off on the second and are met by a 'red cap' who directs us to the spot. Here we wait for two hours and I get orders to collect all cash. This takes time and is in every currency under the sun. I seem to have as much as anyone, having cashed an advance of pay the day before. Again, we move off, this time to a ship. We load all our provisions on to a Greek destroyer – we seem to have a lot, though it is chiefly food and wireless sets and ammunition.

As well as the Greek *Kountouriotis*, the Indian sloop *Sutlej* and the Free French *La Moquese* and *Commandant Dominé* stood by to transport B Squadron, together with other troops, including a detachment of the SBS. At 1830 hours on Sunday, 12 September, the convoy sailed. Initial destination: Kastellorizo. Unbeknown to all except the most senior ranks, this was the beginning of a series of operations that would see mainly British forces dispatched to the Dodecanese in the wake of the Italian armistice. For the LRDG, Phase 11 (Training and Re-equipping) was over. Phase 12 was just beginning.

After another sweltering day onshore, the sudden transition to life at sea was a welcome change. It was also considerably more comfortable for the officers. They were allocated cabins temporarily vacated by their hosts, before being invited for refreshments in their

Mess. It was just one of the privileges of rank. The ORs, of course, had to make do with whatever space was available.

When the convoy had sailed, Lloyd Owen briefed the officers, informing them of their destination: B Squadron was to disembark at Kastellorizo for onward passage in various craft to Leros. Meanwhile, Olivey's sore throat had worsened. He had also developed a temperature and was feeling decidedly unwell. The diagnosis was diphtheria and to Olivey's great disappointment he was required to return to port with the destroyer.

> I am very loathe to leave the Unit, especially as before leaving, my Colonel had called Allen [sic: Captain Alan G. Redfern] and I together and said that in the event of David getting killed, Alan could take over the Squadron and I should take over Alan's patrol. This was a move that suited me, having no skill at organisation and always a hope that I would have a patrol again. I am not sure if Alan was disappointed or not. It gave him promotion which some men seem to like. I do not think the additional pay was considered by either of us. I had an idea that such a move would never happen and felt resigned to my fate. [...]
>
> On the way back, my sleep was disturbed by tremendous thuds over my cabin. I had my suspicions but had never heard a depth charge being released before. The Greek crew were having a great time and fired off forty depth charges, so they said, at this enemy sub. I ventured up on deck to see the fun and found the ocean lit with flares which, I was informed, marked the course of the submarine, which was moving north-west at a slow speed. We crossed and re-crossed over the enemy, but we were running short of depth charges and our fuel was limited on account of a fast run made on the outward journey. No water was to be had, our troops having used rather much. The hunt was kept up for three or four hours, but as far as we could see, without success.

That afternoon, the destroyer arrived at Haifa and Olivey was rushed to hospital. There, his ailment was diagnosed as nothing serious. After being bedbound for several days, Olivey was medically discharged and immediately made his way to the docks to seek passage on the next available ship. The British destroyers *Hurworth* and *Croome* were scheduled to depart some twenty-four hours later. Olivey was allocated one of the ships, this time having to bunk down where he could. He chose the floor under the table of the Officers' Mess, retiring to the upper decks when the ship was underway.

> The day was good and I sat in the sun most of the time having no duties. I have always enjoyed sea trips and the trip on the destroyer was no exception. The sea got a little more rough and by evening, it was blowing hard and a sea running. I had selected a spot on the leeward side and settled down for the night in my sleeping bag and greatcoat. I had been detailed as officer of the port watch. This did not mean very much except that one was responsible that soldiers did not smoke on deck. My responsibility was from 0200–0300 hours. Some hours before this, my sleeping bag was wet through as we seemed to be now running straight into the wind. I went below and again found my pitch under the Mess table. I was called at 0200 hours and sent up on deck. There was no one on deck to smoke so the job was easy enough and my fellow officers and I spent the hour in speculating on the light which we passed on some island or other. I did not again go below as an air raid was in progress on one of the islands and we thought maybe that we should be spotted. We were not, however, and steamed into Leros at 0700 hours.

Olivey arrived at Leros on 17 September, together with the first detachments of the Faughs and the new Fortress Commander, Brigadier F. G. R. 'Ben' Brittorous.

> Breakfast was welcome after a shave and we were casting anchor in the harbour. The Brigadier was going ashore in state as Governor of the Island. The captain of the ship would accompany him. I was standing on deck near the gangway when this event took place. The captain was piped ashore and the Navy saluted. I wondered if I was doing the right thing as none of the other military officers were

at the salute. Again, the pipe blew and this was for the Governor and this time I noticed that everyone was saluting. The Brigadier was obviously pleased, for as I learnt afterwards, saluting was a weakness of his. I think he is right, seeing it is a military order. It shows discipline in the soldier, keeps one alert, and, if done properly, is smart. The Brigadier is, I think, a little out of date. It may be alright in peacetime when the Army is only in uniform on parade and when there are only a few thousand men scattered over the face of the earth. But in war it seems an impossible situation, for in Cairo I had often walked down a street, my hand almost constantly at my cap. Surely, for soldiers to salute officers they know would be quite sufficient in these modern times. The soldiers consider they are being very hardly used in being made to salute, but forget that an officer gives ten for every one of theirs and has to be constantly on the watch not to miss returning a salute. When only half the soldiers salute, this is very difficult. Perhaps we shall see a change in this Army order before long.

George [Major George Jellicoe] came off on one of the boats and told me that David was on the quay and the Unit installed on the islands. I collected my kit together and found a lighter going to shore, so climbed on board. David was on the quay with a jeep. He informed me that the Brigadier had asked for me to be attached to his staff, but I had been saved as David had told him he had important work for me to do – a grand lie!

We move off in the jeep to our quarters which were in the centre of the island and consisted of a Mess of a small two-roomed house shared by David and Dick [medical officer, Captain Richard P. Lawson]. And a wooden hutment in which the patrols were living with one room at the end for officers.

I decided to keep my kit in the room but sleep under the trees near the Mess. The ground had been my bed long enough before and should be again. Mosquitoes were plentiful and nets were used. There seemed no more to be done except to draw the money which had been handed in, change it to local currency with the field cashier and pay it back to the men. The field cashier would not change coppers. He would not, at first, look at Syrian notes. The

> exchange was different for each currency, and needless to say, it was impossible to give back the right exchange. Patrols went away content and returned with many grouses of being short[-changed].

For those who were among the first to arrive on the island of Leros, life was initially peaceful, and for the officers at least, almost idyllic. It was still mid-September, when the weather is warm, sometimes almost unbearably so. Nowhere on Leros is far from the coast with its secluded coves and small beaches where one can soak in the sun and cool off in crystal-clear Aegean waters.

> We spent the afternoons in swimming or fishing, having done what little soldiering we could in the morning. The fish we caught were small, being little layer-thin sardines and the whole catch hardly made a meal for two of us and gave the Mess about a fish each. Alan and I visited a local tavern and tried the local wine which was very poor stuff and we did not go again.

It would be but a brief sojourn. On the same day that Olivey arrived at Leros, a German convoy consisting of the submarine-attack vessel *UJ 2104* and steamers *Pluto* and *Paul* was attacked south of Naxos by eight Beaufighters from Cyprus. In the early hours of 18 September, the convoy was again targeted, this time by shore batteries on Astipalaea, before being attacked by His Majesty's destroyers, *Faulknor* and *Eclipse* and the Greek *Vasilissa Olga* (also called *Queen Olga*). *Pluto* and *Paul* were sunk. *UJ 2104* was damaged and foundered off the east coast of Astipalaea. When initial reports mistakenly indicated that Astipalaea had been invaded, three Italian motor torpedo boats were sent on a fact-finding mission. Two would be written off in an air attack and the third was damaged and beached. After the situation had been clarified, ML (Motor Launch) 355 conveyed four patrols of B Squadron from Leros to Astipalaea, where Lloyd Owen took charge of several German prisoners and returned with them to Leros. The remainder were evacuated shortly afterwards. Before long, all but one of the LRDG patrols on Astipalaea would return to Leros. M2 Patrol under Captain Kenneth H. Lazarus remained to report on enemy aircraft and shipping movements. On 23 September, Olivey was tasked with making a delivery run to the island.

> I just caught the ship and learnt it was not going to the place at which I had orders to meet Ken. Nothing could persuade the skipper to go there, as he was afraid of being bombed. The trip was uneventful and then turned up at the port of call. I handed over the money and we put the mail bag on one side. When we returned for it, someone had moved it and I did not find it until the next morning, too late to give to Ken. Ken's news was that a German destroyer had been bombed and ran aground on the island. The Italians would have handed over the island to the crew, had not Ken and his patrol been there to capture the crew. We brought them back, together with some Italians of a MAS torpedo boat which had been bombed by the Germans. The Rhodesian Patrol returned with Stanley and we left Ken and his patrol on the island.
>
> This was to be the last we saw of Ken, as when asked if he would like to be relieved, he wisely replied that he would rather be bored on his island than bored on ours. But his boredom did not last too long as Jerry captured the island and Ken 'went off the air' about a month later.

Olivey returned to Leros in time for an imminent move to Kalymnos. Glad for an opportunity to operate independently of Brigade, the LRDG, taking with them two of the precious jeeps, embarked on the landing ship *Porto di Roma* the next afternoon, arriving at Kalymnos in the evening.

> What a welcome we received from the Islanders, who went nearly mad and threw their arms around our necks and threw flowers in our faces, saying they had waited twenty years for our coming. The people are very poor with very little to live on. Sponges were the source of income of these people before the war. We gathered that a lot of wealth had been brought back from America. The island

seemed to produce little else, enough for their daily needs, and a few tomatoes and dried fruit.

We occupied a large hospital some little distance from the sea front. Carts were hired to bring the Unit's kit up from the docks and one broken-down taxi augmented the work of the jeeps. The C.O. [the commanding officer at this time was Colonel Guy L. Prendergast] had a great and triumphal going ashore. The flag was hoisted over his quarters and a guard of honour marched through the streets and mounted guard on his quarters, all this, no doubt, to stress English military strength!

The Officers' Mess was a house close by the hospital and here we dug in and made ourselves as comfortable as we could. We bought several gallons of red wine, which was not too bad and was cheap and the only drink we had. Plenty of watermelons and grapes with tomatoes and pumpkins were to be had, as they were imported from the islands.

Swimming in the harbour was the chief sport. David and I took a walk over the mountains and discovered an old nunnery, where we were made welcome and given honey and nuts to eat. One nun fell quite in love with David!

And all the time Leros … Island was being bombed and Kos, an island close to us, was receiving a great hammering as it had two landing grounds which the R.A.F. had occupied.

Leros was bombed for the first time on Sunday morning, 26 September, with Portolago (today, Lakki) the main target. Two destroyers, HMS *Intrepid* and the Greek *Vasilissa Olga* were attacked at their moorings. *Vasilissa Olga* was lost, together with many of her crew. *Intrepid* was seriously damaged and towed inshore, but after being further damaged sank early the next morning. The bombing campaign was to continue for fifty-two days.

Air battles took place daily. We saw many German and our own planes shot down. Pilots came down in parachutes and were usually rescued by fishermen. One German pilot, who was picked up by the doctor of one of our forces, was told a lot of interesting

alright under the Italians and now you are going away and leaving us unprotected – and the Germans bomb our houses and will come and take our men-folk away. Why could you not leave us in peace?" Why not indeed. What could I say but "Despair not, we will be back." For a time I was much depressed – this was the first time I had been in battle where civilians were concerned and the little blue baby and the distraught old lady stayed in my memory for a very long time.'

CHAPTER 3

Clidi

Along with everyone else, John Olivey returned to Leros, disembarking after a short voyage at Portolago.

> We arrived at midnight and it was decided that we should get most of the stuff off the ships straight away, and when landed on the quay, the troops should rest with a small picket to guard the stores. Before leaving Kilmo [sic: Calino/Kaymnos], I had been given a patrol of fifteen or so Rhodesians and we were on picket. I did not feel much like sleep and amused myself with the help of one of the pickets in laying down a 'roller-way' which could be useful for moving the heavy boxes in the morning.

The decision to delay sorting the newly landed stores would have predictable consequences.

> The patrols were all called at first light and everyone worked with a will to get the stores moved off the docks and under cover of the trees. This was just about finished at 0700 hours and breakfast was ready. We all had a very good meal. Just as we had finished, the air-raid alarm sounded and everyone laughed to see the Greeks and Italians run for shelter. We did not laugh for long, however, as it was obvious the raid was intended for us. The planes were chiefly Stukas and came over at about 1,500–2,000 feet. We scattered to what little cover we could find. I, with four or five of my patrol, took cover behind a round cement wall about 4 feet high. Bombs fell all around and shook us badly, the Stukas diving down to about 500 feet before releasing their bombs. They came over in waves

> and in between the waves we moved up into the hills where a pit and slit trench gave us cover.
>
> The raid lasted for about an hour and to many it was their first taste of bombing. One soldier only had been killed. He had been sheltering behind a wall and a bomb had blown the wall over on him. No planes were shot down, as far as I know. Though the A/A [anti-aircraft] had put up a good fire, we had only returned a few rifle shots.

It was Tuesday morning, 5 October, and Portolago had been targeted by twenty-nine Junkers Ju 88s, thirty-four Ju 87s and four Heinkel He 111s. They had dropped a total of 67 tons of high explosive bombs. Captain Thomas E. Belcher was killed, together with Fusilier Colin W. Ashton, Bombardier John Bancroft and Trooper Francis McDaid, all of 30 Commando. Signalman Harold 'Pusher' Wheeldon of the LRDG was mortally wounded.

An unidentified member of the LRDG (probably Lloyd Owen) described the scene:

'The fine streets were a mass of rubble and drooping telephone wires lying across charred and blackened craters. The piles of rations and ammunition were a mass of broken tins and exploded cartridges. Much was still burning and so were many hearts as we saw the quick destruction of so much fine equipment.'

For Olivey and the LRDG, the honeymoon period was well and truly over.

> We were rallied to a patrol point and David then told us to collect our patrols and to move to a certain point in the centre of the island. X2, as my patrol was now called, were the first off the mark. In doing so, I left much of my kit. We left it all in one heap, however, and hoped for the best. On arriving at a crossing on the road, we met the C.O. who informed us that the R.V. [rendezvous] had been changed and that we should move to another spot. I was left to turn back any who were making for the original R.V. I stayed

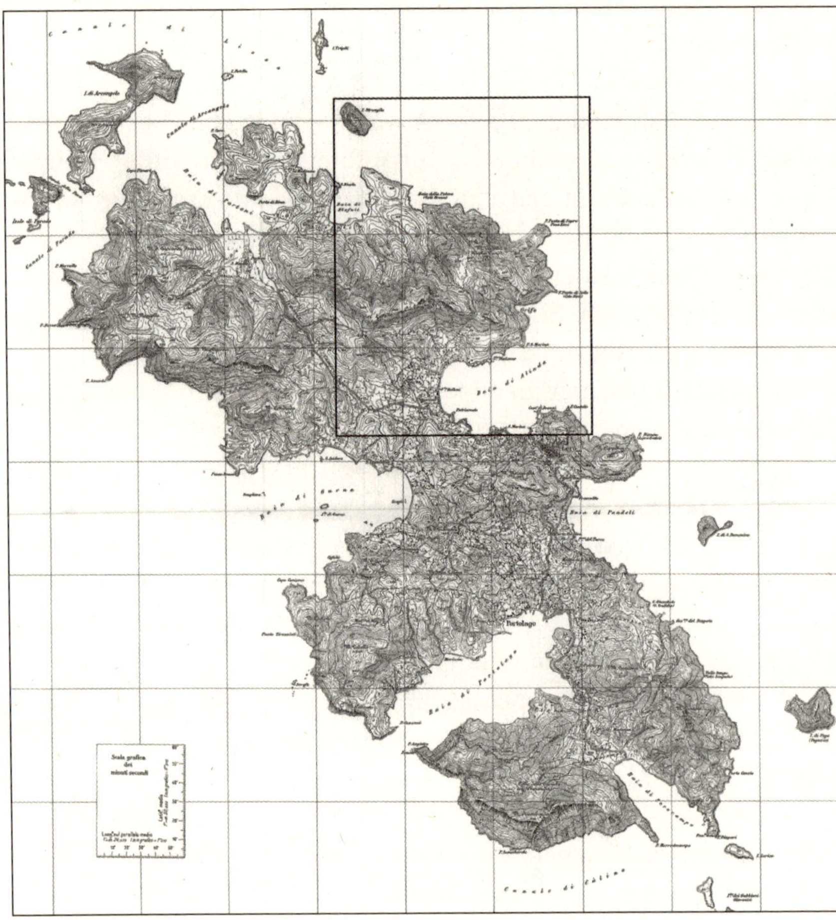
I. di Arcangelo
Canale di Arcangelo
Baia di Parteni
Baia di Alinda
Baia di Gurna
Baia di Pandeli
Portolago
Baia di Portolago

Map 1: Leros

Map 2: Clidi and north-east Leros

> all morning until lunchtime and turned back the whole Unit, more or less! On arriving at the R.V. I found that lunch was ready and immediately afterwards the C.O. was giving us our tasks on the island. My patrol was given the first task as we had been the first to move off. We were to occupy Pt. 320 and to give support to the Italians. We were to boost up their morale, report any approach of shipping or any irregularities with the Italian garrison and to defend the hill if it was attacked. An invasion was expected and tonight seemed a likely night. Transport would pick us up and we were to move off as soon as possible.
>
> We were ready and only had to move down to the road. Again, we were first off the mark. We shared this 5-tonner with another patrol who were to occupy a neighbouring hill. We went up their hill first. The driver was an Italian Marine [more likely a naval rating]. The road was anything but wide, and sitting in front, I often thought the long lorry would never make the bend. The Italian lorries, however, have a wonderful steering and seem to turn, if required, in a circle on their back and we got up this steep path with many hairpin bends and steep drops on one side without accident. Halfway up, two enemy planes flew over. They had bombed elsewhere, however, and we proceeded without trouble. This patrol was delivered and we now progressed down again and up our own road which, if anything, was steeper and more precipitous.

The first patrol had debussed at Battery Farinata, on Mount Marcello (Point 256), in north-west Leros. Olivey with fifteen men was taken to another dominating height just over 3 miles to the east: Mount Clidi (Point 320), site of Battery Ciano, with four 152mm coastal guns and a central command post (CP).

Initially, five patrols were hastened to coastal gun positions: R1 Patrol, commanded by Lieutenant D. J. (Jack) Aitken, R2 (Lieutenant Jack M. Sutherland), X1 (Captain Ronald A. Tinker), X2 (Olivey) and Y2 (Lieutenant John H. Kay). T2 (Second Lieutenant Mervyn W. Cross), Y1 (Captain Moir P. Stormonth Darling) and S2 (Eastwood) were deployed elsewhere on the island. R1, R2 and T2 Patrols (A

Squadron) were situated in the south; S2, X1, X2, Y2 and Y1 Patrols (B Squadron) in the north. T1 Patrol of A Squadron (Captain Charles K. Saxton), and B Squadron's M1 (Folland), M2 (Lazarus) and S1 (Redfern) maintained watch on outlying islands.

The arrangement was fluid and liable to change as the situation dictated. LRDG Advance Headquarters moved into caves at Meraviglia, close to Fortress Headquarters. (Many of the so-called caves on Leros were man-made; some were well-constructed tunnel systems; others served as crude underground shelters.)

Olivey's destination, Battery Ciano, was accessible by a single narrow road cut out of the hillside. This led to a single-storey barrack building and beyond to the gun battery. The battery commander was tenente di artiglieria (artillery lieutenant) Daniele Pieri; his second-in-command was sottotenente di artiglieria (artillery second lieutenant) Ferruccio Pizzigoni.

> We arrived at the Italian barracks at sunset. I found a 2nd Lieutenant Pizzigoni, who spoke French. I told him our orders were to report to the fort and was taken up about 500 yards further on. Here, I met Lieutenant Pr. [Pieri], who commanded the Italian garrison. He showed me round the fort and pointed out trenches and holes dug in the hillside. One I selected for my wireless set. It was a cave blasted out of solid rock and seemed ideal. No bomb could possibly do damage here unless it landed right in the cave. My three signallers agreed it was a good spot and immediately started to move in. We had brought a small charging plant and this was installed in the other cave, which was even better, having been blasted out of solid rock into the shape of a 'Z'.
>
> The first we call 'L' cave and the second 'Z', on account of their shapes. The remainder of my patrol settled down in a trench which also had been blasted out of rock, but had the disadvantage of being right below the muzzles of two of the big guns.

The rocky terrain made it impossible to excavate trenches in the traditional sense. It was common instead to construct stone sangars and defence works.

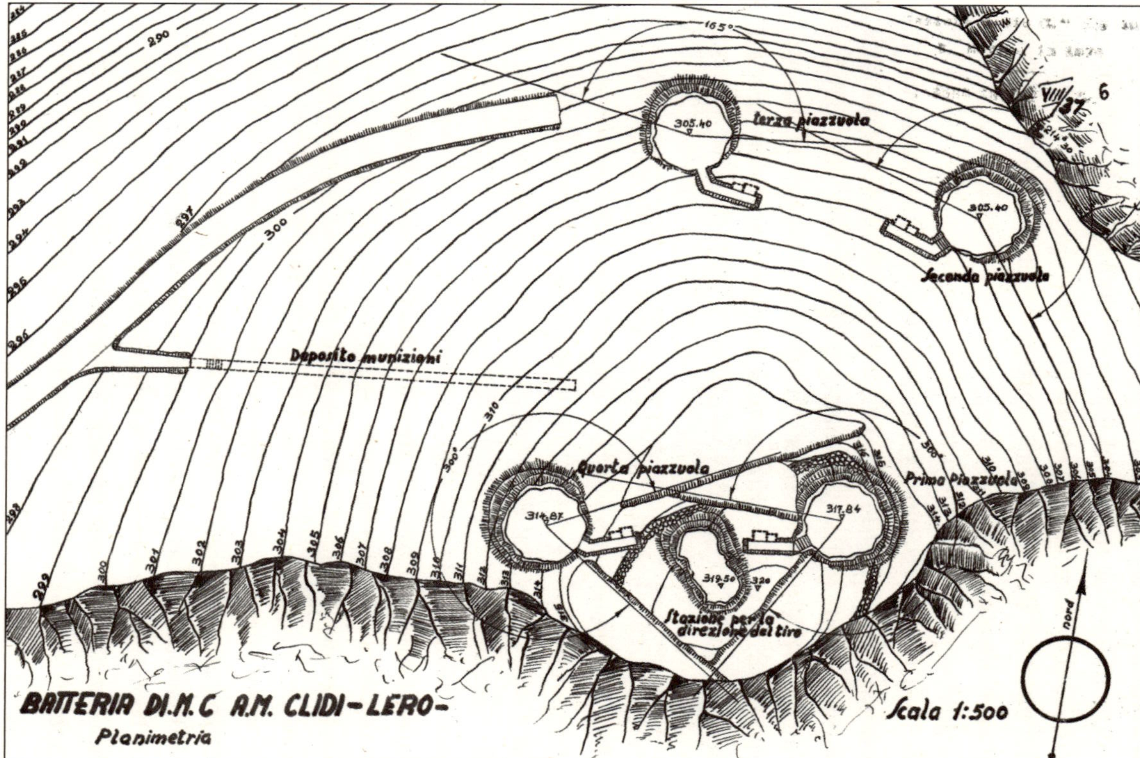

Map 3: Italian plan of Battery Ciano, with numbered gun emplacements 1 (prima) 2 (seconda) 3 (terza), 4 (quarta); command post (stazione per la direzione del tiro) and ammunition depot (deposito munizioni). (*General State Archives, Rhodes*)

We posted two men to be on lookout constantly, the watch being changed every two hours, and these reported every light for miles around so that I was kept up nearly all night. Some rocks, which formed islands varying from a mile to 5 miles out at sea, looked like landing craft with waves breaking over their bows. The Italians, some of whom have served at this fort for five or more years, could not, of course, see the approaching craft we pointed out and must have thought us very windy!

Daylight brought us better organisation, however. The men had moved off with only one blanket each and we now got an issue of Tropal coats, which we preferred to sleeping bags. These sleeping bags of the Unit are grand, being made of down and very warm. They are rather unserviceable to protect one while standing on guard at night, whereas the Tropal coats with their sheepskin lining, oilskin and canvas cover are serviceable as blankets, coats or anything else.

The full-length Tropal coat, of khaki canvas, with a serge collar and quilted kapok lining, had gained popularity with the LRDG during the desert war.

We had food for three days with us and water for about the same period. We elected one of our members as cook, another as Q.M. [quartermaster], my Lance Corporal took charge of supplies and we were getting organised. Lance Corporal C. [Donald T. Coventry] was a grand stand-by throughout our stay at 320. He could speak a little Greek. I nicknamed him 'Ox' because this Fort Victoria boy was mighty tough, though slow of thinking.

Pt. 320 was revealed in the morning as an almost sheer rock mound rising about 1,000 feet above the sea. It commanded a complete view to the north with the exception of the north-west corner, where we had left the other patrol. In the north were two large bays about 2 miles distant as the crow flies, and various islands further north as far as the eye could see. All these islands were occupied by Italians, and the principal one, Samos, had a few British troops on it latterly. The coast swung round to the east,

> passing a cove with steep sides and a sandy beach on the southern end and disappeared from our view by a high hill. Part of our position, this hill was continued after a short neck by a hill to the east. Through the neck one caught a glimpse of the sea somewhat closer, but still not of the coast.

Parteni is a sizeable anchorage nearly 2 miles to the north-west. Blefuti Bay, considerably smaller, lies east of Parteni and just over a mile from Clidi. What Olivey describes as a 'cove with steep sides' is Palma Bay, about 700 yards east of Blefuti and almost due north of Clidi. The ground then steadily rises to a series of hills along the northern coast, the highest of which is Point 264 (Mount Vedetta).

A ridge with prominent twin peaks – Point 278 – extends east from Clidi to the coast and Grifo Bay – hidden from view due to the undulating ground between the twin peaks and Vedetta.

Clidi also overlooks much of the terrain to the south, and as such was to become what was probably the most important battle position on the island. Olivey's description continues:

> There was, therefore, about a mile of the coast which was completely hidden from view and on which we could, therefore, bring no fire to bear. Besides this, the Fort Commander had pointed out that his guns would not depress to the cove [described] above. Our trench overlooked this bay, however, and it was in range of Bren gun fire. The Italians had three .300 machine guns trained on this area. To the south lay a large and important bay [Alinda] with the shore almost making a circle, all within range of our Bren guns. The centre of the island, a narrow strip of land, nearly flat, connected this bay with another [Gurna] to the south-west, this bay [being] about 1½ [miles] distant and [with] the coast passing out of view to the north-west and south, glimpses being caught again further south. One hill was connected to the north-west by a narrow strip of land up which the road had brought us, but some very rocky ground and descending out of view to the north-west. The northern approaches were passable, though steep, and the Italians guarded them with barbed wire. The north-west approach was

> very steep and impassable in places, besides having one trench overlooking it. The east slope had a path which steeply wound its way up the hill, passing close to the Z trench and above the L and arriving on top between two stones [sic] constructed trench walls and under the muzzle of No. 1 gun. The south side was sheer rock, impassable. It was quite obvious from the start that No. 1 gun was the centre of the fort's life. Everything happened from No. 1 gun. It was closest to the fort, commanded the best view of the coast to the north and east and south, was the best kept gun and the position of the rangefinder made the gun most accurate. No. 2 gun was to the west and commanded a view of the island to the south, with a dead area to the east, but a good view to the north-east and north. No. 3 gun was just below No. 1 and to the north east, and No. 4 gun on a level with No. 3 but immediately north. No. 3 and 4 guns had no view to the south. All guns were connected to the fort by telephone. The fort was right on the top and consisted of a two-storey pillbox, the lower room, being the control room, was below ground and connected by a Z-shaped passage from the north.

Olivey correctly identifies No. 1 gun, but for the remaining three guns he applied a numbering system at odds to that used by the Italians. He refers to No. 4 gun as No. 2, No. 2 as No. 3 and No. 3 as No. 4. The 'fort' was an elevated structure with all-round cover and served as the battery control post and an observation platform.

> To get to the upper room, one climbed a rung ladder and appeared through a 2-foot square hole in the floor into a round room with horizontal slit windows to the east, north and west. This room had a diameter of about 15 feet with wings out to the windows, east and west. A ramp of stone ran up to the north side of this [---] and arrived on top of an earth circle which buried the [---] to a depth of 2 feet, and, with stones around the sides and base, made it almost bomb proof, though I doubt if it would have stood up to a direct hit from a 500-pounder. The guns were all old naval guns of Italian construction dated 1899–1904. The shells were in

two parts and were kept in a large or main magazine 100 yards to the west of No. 4 gun, or for immediate use, shells and shell cases were stored in individual magazines on the hillside in easy reach of each gun. All guns swung through 360 degrees and had a range of approximately 5 miles, so we were told. Each had a shield of mild steel for protection of its crew, who could sit and range their gun through a telescope. A crew of about fifteen men went to each gun. The telescopes were good in most cases and better than our binoculars, especially with their [reticle?] hairlines, pointing out targets which we could not explain in Italian or French. The rangefinder was a long strip of rounded tube about 9" thick and 15' long. I never looked through this rangefinder but it looked as though it should be most accurate according to its size. Beside this was a small plate for bearings, cleverly but simply arranged so that the observer lined up a hairline with a slit and read the bearing in front of him. We found this most useful for giving true bearings.

The fort was connected to the island commander's H.Q. by telephone and also to the neighbouring forts and a searchlight which operated due north. All batteries could give each other covering fire if required.

Besides this was a 7mm Scotti, which was our A/A gun and fired small H.E. [high explosive] shells in clips of ten. It had a range of about 3,000 feet and a proportion of the shells were tracer. The gunner sat on the gun and directed it either with foot on the ground or with a hand control and elevated with a hand control, firing either by foot or by hand. We had put these guns on some of our trucks in the desert and a few of us knew how unreliable they could be if not kept clean. The Italians obviously knew this also as the gun was always clean and the shells always well-oiled in their clips.

The Scotti, mentioned several times by Olivey, may have been confused with another weapon type, possibly the 8x59mm Breda Mod. 37, with a side-fed twenty-round magazine .

The patrol arms were not very considerable. Our role, for which we had trained, being to move round or through the enemy lines and there receive supply droppings or explosives, or otherwise to report on our particular job by wireless back to H.Q., we now found ourselves in an infantry job with reporting on shipping, for which we were hardly trained. I had very little idea of the tonnage of ships and my men were Rhodesians who, except for holidays, some of them at Durban or Cape Town, had hardly seen the sea. We found ourselves equipped with a wireless set and a Bren gun, a box of magazines, a rifle or revolver per man and a box of grenades and a Verey pistol for signalling. We were fairly well equipped with telescopes, binoculars, compasses and a map of the island.

We made ourselves very agreeable to the Italians. I insisted that anyone passing the commandant should salute him. I myself missed no opportunity in giving him every compliment I could. This very man brought his reward as he, seeing I was in a somewhat exposed position, kindly lent me a tarpaulin which I fixed up over my stone emplacement to make a tent and camouflage as best I could, using stones and bush with a sprinkling of earth. This gave me cover from the dew at night and allowed the use of a candle for writing messages. I had arranged a series of whistle signals for calling signallers and I then had to shout the message down to them. This was not easy as there was usually a high wind blowing on top of this hill, but it was the best we could devise in view of having no telephone. Later, we did try to fix up a rope on which to pass messages, but it was too slow and not a success. Shipping reports were all sent in a pre-arranged sequence of direction, position and size of ship, etc., and then passed over the air in code. As the navy did not tell us the movement of ships, no doubt a number of our ships were reported unnecessarily and we were kept busy reporting.

About the second day, I had a visit from George Jellicoe who informed me that his plan was to withdraw through our position and that he was leaving some boxes of provisions and water somewhere nearby. We had this on, rather I should say, we moved these close to our lines, so that we could keep a watch on them, but I warned George that we were in no way responsible for their safety.

During the first two or three days, the Germans were very active with their bombers and they would visit the island three or four times each day, usually selecting to drop their bombs on Brigade H.Q. [Meraviglia] and close to our H.Q. It seemed that at least two bombers in each raid were selected to pick out other localities and we came in for our full share of these. I had found rather a good position to sit and rest in the afternoon. It consisted of a 3-foot ledge just below the signal cave with a sheer rock of about 6 feet high above it and a sheer drop below. I considered this the safest spot on the island, not having a liking for caves and the like which I find are inclined to make one more frightened than they are worth. I much prefer a sudden end, to being shut in a cave by a fallen rock, but these are not everyone's failings and my troops, I fancied, thought I was mad to sit in the rain! I had not, I think, considered machine-gun fire from the aircraft and relied rather on them not noticing me. I spent many good hours with a book, the only English book the Italians had, in this position and obtained some very good photographs of the village being bombed and dust rising from the area of H.Q.

Photographs taken by Allied troops on Leros are almost non-existent. What of those taken by Olivey? A few years after the end of the war, he disclosed to another former LRDG officer, Stanley A. 'Stuka' Stokes: 'I fear I lost most of my snaps in Leros where I buried them and no doubt they are useless now as they were never developed.'

At this stage, no-one except our A/A gun fired back at the aircraft, chiefly, I think, because of shortage of ammunition. An occasional rifle shot was fired, however.

The C.O. [Brittorous] visited me on the third day and I was able to report that we were more or less settled in. I asked for blankets, more grenades, and if possible, an E.Y. grenade cap. These caps fit on the end of a rifle and a grenade slips into them – they are fired by a ballistic cartridge, rather like a blank and can then shoot the grenade on level ground about 300 yards. I had fancied my chance with one of these and four-second fused grenades for firing at low-flying aircraft. None to be had, however, and I was never able to try my luck. It must be remembered in all these firing operations at aircraft that we were 1,000 feet above everyone else, and thus the aircraft were often in range to us when out of range of other troops on the island.

Having reported and thought all well, the C.O. had a few things to say. My cap badge had not been cleaned, and I would see that all troops cleaned their cap badges. I glanced at his and he remarked that he knew his was not clean either! I had not looked at it, however, and my glance was quite unconscious. He also remarked that our sentries were on watch in shorts only, having taken off their shirts in the sun. If they had arms, they were not obviously present, and for all these things I received a rocket. The polished Brasso rocket had rather knocked me for a loop and I failed to 'take in' much more of the visit. I did ask for cotton wool for our ears and had considered asking for Brasso but thought this sounded too cheeky, and, after all, even C.O.s may get a bit het-up with air raids and bombs, and I expect he had had more than I in his H.Q.

I passed on all these rockets and from that moment on, my cap badge was ever shining, though some of the men, I noticed, preferred to lose theirs, thinking perhaps that the glint attracted bullets!

The blankets and grenades arrived in due course and we used mud for 'Brasso'.

On Sunday, about the fourth [sic] day, I received my kit which Jake had collected from Q. [quartermaster]. With this was everything I could possibly require, clean kit, shaving kit, towels, socks and even 'Daraghit' [sic: presumably Duraglit metal cleaner], which I always carried around with me. I had an excellent shave and a wash and felt a thousand times better. I encouraged Kevan [Trooper John D. 'Flossie' Kevan] to come for a walk with me down to the shore where we would have a swim, search out a good R.V. and visit B. Squadron, who had camped in the broken country west of us. We had an excellent walk and swim, dried in the sun and started back, up the hill to B. Squadron. We found David and his merry men well hidden in the trees and bushes and his H.Q.

> well concealed in the rocks. We received a little medical attention from Dick Lawson who was also there with Stanley and Stormy [Stormonth Darling]. David did explain their role which, as far as I could see, consisted of remaining hidden till after the battle, then prancing out or getting off the island, whichever seemed to suit the occasion! I suggested that a few dummy gun emplacements in spots where there were no troops would draw bombs away from other areas, but David had other ideas. I collected a few cigarettes and – joy of joys – a bottle of Haig. Kevan had started back with the cigarettes as he was due for lookout and was late. I stayed talking a while, had a cup of tea and a biscuit and chocolate and after waiting for a raid to pass over, left the camp.

Aircraft were still overhead, but as the raid appeared to be directed elsewhere, Olivey considered it safe to return to Clidi.

> I walked on up the road after shouting back to B. Squadron that "The Stukas will get you, if you don't look out!" rather giving the song some local colour! I had just got beyond the Italian barracks when it was quite obvious that the raid was coming our way. David had told me the sad story of how one of the men had picked up a case of whisky on the docks. A raid had taken place so that he had put the whisky down and taken cover. When he returned, his precious case had had a direct hit. Everyone, as soldiers will, asked why he had not placed the case in cover and himself stayed there!
>
> So, thinking of the whisky, I made for the drain which ran down the side of the road and lay down in it, thereby feeling more or less safe. The raid was certainly for us. One Ju 88 dipped at the fort and finished its run over me. Bombs fell all around and chiefly on the fort. There was a tremendous explosion, followed by several others and men came running out of the fort. The explosions continued and it was quite obvious that one of the magazines had been struck.
>
> I went up onto a rocky hillside 200 yards west of the fort and then proceeded to collect my men. They all came along one after another. B. Squadron, however, hearing my shouts, thought that I

> was calling for assistance as the explosions were very great now. It appears and appeared later, when we could get close enough to the fort, that No. 1 gun had had a direct hit. It was most impressive, and no doubt the Jerry pilot has since got his Iron Cross, as the bomb had dropped right on the barrel of the gun, cutting it completely in two and wrecking the gun on its mounting. Another bomb had dropped in No. 1 gun's magazine and set it on fire. There were marks of bombs below on the hillside and stringing right back to my position. The Germans had certainly had luck.
>
> We waited nearby for some two hours while the explosions continued. It seemed there had been no casualties, though Coventry had been standing on the gun mount at the time. He had taken a flying jump over the top, and in so doing, saved his life. His rifle, which was resting against the gun, was blown to bits, as were also the binoculars and compass, which were close by. The rangefinder had been destroyed and generally this gun position had been demolished. The magazine burnt and exploded till dark. Two Italians had returned to the gun and had entered the magazine rather too soon. A loud explosion killed one and mortally wounded the other.

Writing in the third person, Don Coventry also recalled events, with a tongue-in-cheek reference to his OC's oft-mentioned exhortation to his men to maintain faith:

'Captain Olivey was called to HQ and Lance Corporal Coventry was left in charge. Coventry, with Mackay [Private John 'Daisy' MacKay] from Y Patrol, were on guard next to one of the big Naval guns when eight Junkers 88s attacked from the Turkish coast. Having faith, we remained at our post. The Junkers dived and dropped their bombs, which missed. They then turned and came back out of the afternoon sun and did another run.

'I was watching through the binoculars and the bomb seemed to be coming straight down the lens. I shouted to Mackay to take cover and we jumped over the Dannert wire and slid down the slope into a cave where our wireless operators were.

'The bomb scored a direct hit on the Naval gun, chopped the barrel clean off and tilted the gun out of the ground. The explosion set fire to the gun's magazine.

'At this time, unbeknown to us, Flossie Kevan was coming along to have a chat and, being a bit hard of hearing, saw us leap over the wire, so he crouched down on a ledge below the Naval gun where we found him afterwards, covered in stones and earth but, miraculously, alive. He was temporarily totally deaf and shocked from the explosion.

'With all this I had forgotten my .303 leaning against the Naval gun and all that I found of it afterwards was the breech and bolt.'

Unsurprisingly, 'Flossie' Kevan never forgot his lucky escape:

'I was overtaken by a raid which caused me to take cover under a rock about twenty feet below the targets. I could see bombs going down the valley and also the compression waves as they exploded but suddenly there was an almighty crash … and I was buried under large chunks of rock and at the same time lost my hearing completely. This latter was temporary, thank Goodness, though irreparable damage was done. I was pulled out otherwise and unexpectedly intact and returned to duty which involved the rescue of our radio from the smouldering bunker after which John Olivey produced a bottle of whisky from behind his back which helped enormously.'

As for No. 1 gun: 'John Olivey got us to rig up the huge range-finder as a replacement barrel which would look convincing from the air – and no doubt attracted even more dive-bombing.'

Olivey continues:

> The C.O. visited us and we were able to report no casualties amongst our number at the time. He had thought to find heavy casualties, I believe. When we had all collected, I considered it a good time to broach the bottle. We each took a mouthful. What a drink. I had never tasted better in my life and kept the raw spirit milling round my palate for a good two minutes, while my mind rushed back to friends at home and numerous great occasions

when I had enjoyed a drink in friends' company. That mouthful certainly did me good and only those who have been revived after a long stretch on a hot afternoon in the middle of an air raid can possibly appreciate how I felt.

We slowly moved back to our trench, had dinner and took up positions around the hill. I would not allow my troops onto the top as the magazine was still burning, with explosions every now and then.

The Italians were taking the night off but were perhaps jealous of us remaining, as the commander sent me a message just after I had fallen to sleep, to say that the main magazine was thought to be on fire and there was serious danger of the hilltop being blown completely off – a gross exaggeration, as I discovered later. We moved a little further down the hill, however, and then moved the wireless set down, Coventry and van Heerden [Rifleman L. J. 'Vic' van Heerden] going back to bring this down at what then seemed great risk. The wireless set got damaged in the move and we were unable to signal in any case. Before nightfall, I had received several messages to the effect that 'tonight was the night' meaning the night of the invasion, no doubt. How many more times I was to receive this warning!

My Lance Corporal Ox had done very well. He had, immediately after the gun had been hit, sent a wireless message stating what had happened, also reporting the movement of two ships, and at the same time advising that the wireless set was closing down for a short while on my orders.

Early next morning, I returned to the top of the hill. I found that the fire was almost out in the magazine and that an Italian was standing at each of the remaining guns.

The troops moved the wireless set back up the hill and I cleaned out my dug-out. The hole had been almost completely filled in with loose rocks and earth. The tarpaulin had been torn and was now more or less useless. Maps and papers had been blown away. My compass was never seen again. My pipe and binoculars were safe, although a prism had been damaged in the binoculars. I felt thankful I had not been in the hole at the time.

We now hoisted a 'tin hat' on a pole above the fort to show Jerry that our flag still flew. This tin hat remained on this pole for some weeks, until a strong wind blew it off and it became neglected.

The Italians spent the morning burying their dead. They explained that they were their first casualties, and naturally it took them somewhat hard. I paid a visit to the commander's quarters and offered our felicitations. Later in the day, 2nd Lieutenant Pizzigoni came up to the fort and I took a photograph of him standing by one of the guns and then standing near the destroyed No. 1 gun. He also took one of some of my chaps and I.

It was about this time that we commenced our propaganda campaign. We stacked up notices everywhere, encouraging the weak to greater things, in the style of there in the Western Desert.

One which I drew out with great care and stuck up on top of the fort depicted an old time British soldier marked 'Uncle Bill' marching with his sword in a supposed photograph. Another, a supposed photograph of Mafeking on a very low mound of a hill. It read "It was with men like these – on hills like these – that Mafeking was held!"

I had attached to me five British gunners who were there to blow the guns if we had to abandon the position. The above compliment to the British Army obviously pleased them, coming from Rhodesians as it did.

During the day, several Jerry aircraft flew over to see their handiwork.

Our own Beaufighters used to circle the coast each morning, looking for landing craft. It gladdened our hearts considerably. These planes would dive out of a cloud almost to sea level and so do their patrol. A number of M.L.s were on the station and these used to patrol at night and hide up during the day in any crevice or overhanging rock they could find. Unfortunately, some of the camouflage was not as good as others and Jerry sometimes spotted them and would then bomb them for all he was fit. He did not seem to machine-gun them much at this stage, and they were small enough targets in any case.

We had boosted the Italian morale sky-high and one day the Italian commander offered me the use of the top room in his fort. This was excellent and I moved in straight away, making myself a desk out of grenade boxes and hanging my maps on the wall for easy reference. I made myself very comfortable in this little tower, putting my bed, which I borrowed from the Italians, in one alcove and my desk on one side of the room. I had Kevan, who acted as interpreter, speaking better French than I did, living in the same room. I connected the C.O. and we decided the wireless set would be better in this fort, being close at hand for reports and more comfortable for the signallers. They set up their aerial along the top of the fort and got excellent results. The charging engine was kept just below No. 1 gun so everything was very handy. Only a direct hit would put us out of action.

I requisitioned for and obtained sandbags for the windows and closed these up to small slits.

Our days always commenced with stand-to at break of day until sunrise, and everyone knew his position. I myself used to take up my position on top of the fort and from there could see everything for miles around.

Stand-to can be a most inspiring business under such circumstances and standing in silence on top of the tower with the world, as it were, at my feet, brought many thoughts to my mind. I used to feel my ancestors standing behind me. Bishop de Rotheram would whisper a prayer in my ear and I think his first prayer inspired me most – it was simply: "If ye have faith as a grain of mustard seed, ye shall move mountains", and from this time on, I made this my creed. I had faith greater than mustard seed and argued my troops to have the same.

Here, John Olivey alludes to sharing an impressive lineage of historical figures. Bishop de Rotheram [sic] is presumably the fifteenth-century English cleric and statesman Thomas Rotherham, who had been bishop of several dioceses, Archbishop of York, and twice served as Lord Chancellor.

> Captain Rotheram, who was, so I am told, captain of Nelson's 'Victory', used to give me great courage, and Captain Olivey, who died at the last stand at Maward against the Mad Mullah, I felt was also there. It was all most inspiring. My thoughts used to fly the ocean to my darlings in Africa and I could almost hear Mick [Mary Olivey] listening on her set. I hope she could hear my little prayers for her welfare.

Captain Edward Rotheram came to prominence during the Battle of Trafalgar while commanding Vice Admiral Cuthbert Collingwood's flagship *Royal Sovereign*. It would appear that in his reference to Captain Olivey and Maward [sic], John Olivey has confused two siblings. In the first two decades of the twentieth century, British forces in the Somaliland Protectorate were fiercely opposed by Dervishes led by Sayyid Muhammad Abdullah Hassan, aka the 'Mad Mullah'. Captain Herbert E. Olivey, 1st Battalion The Suffolk Regiment attached to 2nd Battalion The King's African Rifles, was killed in Somaliland on 17 April 1903. An older brother, Second Lieutenant Walter R. Olivey, 66th (Berkshire) Regiment of Foot, was killed at the Battle of Maiwand, Afghanistan, on 27 July 1880.

> The room in the fort gave me plenty of time to write letters and I think I wrote to most of my friends in these few weeks, though whether the letters ever arrived, I cannot say, as the journey was very perilous, through enemy waters. We used to receive mail occasionally, either by destroyer or perhaps by aircraft, which used to drop supplies at night. Many tons of stuff were dropped in this way by D.C. [DC-3/C-47 Dakota] and I hoped the Eureka I had collected from Ramat David had come in useful.
>
> I fed with the men in their trench and the food was cooked by one lad who had taken it on as his job, thereby being excused guards, etc. The only British Tommy with us at that time took on Q's job and did it excellently. Water we used to buy from a Greek who came round with two donkeys and filled our cans. He also took washing, both of which were paid for twice a week. He did

not iron, however, and we always tried to get someone to iron the washing, but without success.

So the weeks passed by, with bombing most days, but this we were used to now and hardly noticed.

I had had attached to me Corporal Thomas Bradfield, a very sound Rhodesian with good organising ability. He and Coventry were great friends and both should have had commissions, I felt. Thomas wanted to see a submarine – why, I can't think. I told him if he had faith even this was possible. Early in the morning next day, sure enough, [there] appears a submarine just off our headland. This was obviously one of ours as, on a given signal, a boat put out to meet it. It submerged again shortly after, but Thomas had seen his submarine. A few days later, during the night and while an air raid was in progress, another submarine surfaced in a spot where no searchlight could touch it. It shortly afterwards submerged, appearing again a few hours later at the same spot for a few minutes. I have never been able to find out if this was enemy or not, but sent Coventry down to the hills in front to see if he could see any strangers on the hills. He reported nothing unusual, and as H.Q. did not appear to be in any way interested, I left it at that.

CHAPTER 4

Olympos Convoy and His Majesty's Schooner *Hedgehog*

After the successful operation to seize Kos, Generalleutnant Friedrich-Wilhelm Müller, commanding 22. Infanteriedivision, prepared for Operation *'Leopard'* – the assault on Leros – using essentially the same troops. Before his front-line units could be redeployed, however, they had to be relieved. Accordingly, on Wednesday, 6 October, IX./Festungsinfanteriebataillon (IX Fortress Infantry Battalion) embarked on the steamship *Olympos* and six *Marinefährprahme* (*MFP*, or F-lighter) and departed Piraeus, escorted by the submarine-hunter *UJ 2111*. The vessels were spotted by Allied aircraft soon afterwards. An enemy report was also transmitted by T1 Patrol of the LRDG from an observation post (OP) on Kythnos in the Cyclades. At 0401 hours on the 7th, His Majesty's Submarine *Unruly* sighted the convoy off Kos. Exactly one hour later she fired four torpedoes, all of which missed. *Unruly* surfaced and at 0600 crewmen brought into action her deck gun, firing in all fifty-four high explosive rounds. *Olympos* and an *MFP* were struck; the former veered away and the latter was set on fire and immobilised.

When the convoy came under fire from the port side, the escort vessel led the five remaining *MFP* in taking avoiding action by turning to starboard. German air support was called for, although the attacker had not yet been identified. Minutes later, the escort vessel began taking hits. It was not until first light, some sixteen minutes after the first shots were fired, that two submarines were reported on the surface, close to Levitha, and more than 4½ miles away. *UJ 2111* and one *MFP* engaged. One submarine was seen to emit smoke; the other dived. There was no longer any sign of either *Olympos* or the damaged landing craft. *UJ 2111* and the five *MFP* therefore continued at speed towards Kos.

Meanwhile, an enemy report by *Unruly* had alerted the Royal Navy cruisers *Sirius* and *Penelope* in company with the destroyers *Faulknor* and *Fury*. The destroyers intercepted and sank *Olympos* before rejoining the cruisers and concentrating on the rest of the convoy.

As the British warships appeared through the morning mist, *UJ 2111* opened fire. The warships responded by pairing off for a flanking attack. *UJ 2111* fired at the cruisers, before the hopelessness of the situation prompted the order to divert to Astipalaea, hoping to use the coast as cover. It was too late. While the cruisers focused on the submarine-hunter, the destroyers turned their guns on the landing craft. *UJ 2111* swerved as shells landed some 200 yards on either side. The situation on board was desperate. The vessel was severely damaged, and with so much shrapnel covering the decks it was impossible to carry ammunition forward to the last remaining gun. As the opposing forces closed to 750 yards, the order was given to scuttle *UJ 2111* and abandon ship.

During the engagement, the cruisers had been subjected to air attack by Ju 88s and fired at by a shore battery on Astipalaea, albeit without effect. At 0810 the unit turned south-east and departed at speed, firing at those who had left their sinking vessels and were now struggling helplessly in the sea.

Only the badly damaged *F 496* survived to reach Astipalaea. On board were at least eighty personnel, three trucks and two 7.5cm guns, all of which were captured by Italian troops and the LRDG M2 Patrol.

Operation '*Leopard*' was to have gone ahead on 9 October irrespective of the destruction of the *Olympos* convoy. Mainly due to continued sightings of British warships and unsuitable weather conditions, however, there would be ongoing delays for the next four weeks. What no one could have foreseen was the extraordinary series of events that had been set in motion. These were to have serious and lasting repercussions for the LRDG. Destined for a lead role in the unfolding drama was an old steam trawler.

On 14 October, His Majesty's Schooner *Hedgehog* departed Leros. 'Hedgers', as she was generally known, had been acquired from Haifa in 1941 and initially taken on charge by the para-naval section of Special Operations Executive, under command of Major Stanley E. Beckinsale. She would later join the Levant Schooner Flotilla. In his book, *Dust upon the Sea*, W. E. Benyon-Tinker described the vessel thus:

'*Hedgehog*, a sixty-ton iron-built ex-fishing boat, had come from Alexandria stuffed with odd stores (carried in what used to be the fish refrigerator) and was to be attached to us as general utility ship and maid of all work. She was a brute to steer; rolled like a pig in any sea; had a maximum speed forward of four knots and nothing at all astern – unless there was a head wind blowing, when she promptly went astern with snipe-like rapidity; and was generally battered and worn with great age. Some extremists among us stated that she had started life as a trireme but that was generally believed to be a little exaggerated.'

Hedgehog was now under the command of Sub-Lieutenant David N. Harding, who had been tasked with supplying M2 Patrol of the LRDG on Astipalaea. Harding's instructions stated:

'On arrival at Stampalia you are to land the provisions and stores and contact the Italian Commander with a view to bringing back wounded P.O.W's [prisoners of war]. A maximum of ten P.O.W's (unwounded) who should be officers and N.C.O's [non-commissioned officers] primarily, are to be brought back as well as any wounded, who have first priority.'

In all, more than fifty prisoners were embarked.

Soon after 0600 hours on 16 October, HMS/M *Surf* reported sighting a 'caique'. The submarine fired two warning shots. A light flashed in reply, signalling 'English' and then 'Hedgehog', which only served to confuse matters. Another shot was fired, following which *Surf* approached and at last recognised *Hedgehog*. The engine had ceased, and so the boat was taken in tow towards Levitha. A low-flying aircraft was then sighted, whereupon *Surf* slipped the tow and dived to avoid detection. When the submarine surfaced seventeen minutes later, *Hedgehog* was seen to be operating under her own steam and so was left to proceed independently.

What followed is outlined in a report by Lieutenant Commander L. F. (Frank) Ramseyer on Leros:

'The P.O.W. in Stampalia were embarked in H.M.L.S. HEDGEHOG, but numbers well in excess of those laid down in the orders were included.

'The first sign of trouble was a signal from Sub Lt. Harding via the Italian W/T [wireless telegraphy, or radio] in Levita that "HEDGEHOG" had engine trouble. Later in the day signal reports were made regarding "HEDGEHOG's" condition.

'At the time no craft was available to send that night, and 48 hours elapsed before an M.L. finally reached Levita. In the interim the enemy had apparently overpowered the small British guard and Italian garrison. H.M.S. "HEDGEHOG" was observed burning in the harbour, but no contact could be established with her crew ashore.

'Odd reports indicate that German seaplane visited Levita and in all probability evacuated the captured British and Italian troops.'

How or when *Hedgehog* caught fire is just one of several unexplained occurrences in the story of Levitha. Neither is it known how or when German prisoners were able to seize the initiative and report their plight. Of significance, perhaps, is an entry in the War Diary of the Kriegsmarine: 'According to radio intelligence, the Italian radio station on Levitha received orders in the afternoon to offer resistance under all circumstances and to destroy code material in case of danger.'

Whatever had happened, German command had been made aware by Sunday, 17 October. That evening, Oberleutnant Oschatz, commanding 15. Kompanie (Fallschirmjäger)/4. Regiment 'Brandenburg' (15./4.Rgt. 'Brandenburg'), was tasked to prepare an assault force to secure Levitha and rescue their fellow countrymen. In the meantime, a Leutnant Fickers had already arrived at Levitha in an Arado seaplane. Before long, the officer had established contact with his countrymen at Vurcalo inlet.

Early the next morning, the paratroopers were transported from Athens-Phaleron in two Junkers Ju 52 seaplanes and a Dornier flyingboat, with three AR 196 Arados as escort and three providing forward reconnaissance. After their transports had alighted on the sea just off Levitha, the men prepared rubber dinghies for the short trip ashore. In the event, one of the inflatables capsized and an occupant was dragged under water, weighted down by ammunition boxes and equipment. He was to be the only German fatality.

According to the unit after-action report, the landing and subsequent sweep through the island was unopposed. Nonetheless, an Italian building atop Point 130 (Segnale), variously described as a radio station and a meteorological station, was strafed and bombed by Arados. Two Italians there were fatally wounded; the remainder fled. At least one of those taken prisoner, Petty Officer Hubert V. Bevan, was also wounded, presumably when the German prisoners had taken control of *Hedgehog*.

Contact was established with the German prisoners and by 1330, just four and a half hours after their arrival, Oschatz's paratroopers had achieved their objective.

All nine crewmembers of *Hedgehog*, including two Greeks, and eleven Italians from Levitha were taken prisoner. In the afternoon of 18 October, the crew of *Hedgehog* was evacuated. It is not known what became of the Italians. Most of the assault group departed after being relieved by troops of 11. Kompanie/Luftwaffen-Jägerregiment 21 (11./Lw.-Jg.Rgt.21). The remaining Brandenburger left by Ju 52 the next day. *Hedgehog* was abandoned at Vurcalo inlet.

On Friday morning, 22 October, 15./4.Rgt. 'Brandenburg' was dropped at Maltezana, Astipalaea. The paratroopers were followed by 1. Kompanie/1. Regiment 'Brandenburg' (1./1.Rgt. 'Brandenburg'), who arrived in seaplanes before coming ashore in inflatables. As they advanced, the Germans freed forty-eight German prisoners, most if not all of whom were from the ill-fated *Olympos* convoy. By 1400 hours the Germans were in control of the island.

M2 Patrol commander Lazarus was one of the few to escape captivity. He reached Haifa on 8 December.

On Saturday, 23rd, the day after radio contact had ceased between Astipalaea and Leros, an Axis radio broadcast announced that Axis prisoners of war on Levitha had overpowered their captors. It was decided, presumably by Middle East Command, if not by Brittorous, to mount a seaborne operation to rid Levitha of enemy forces. The LRDG were saddled with the task, which was to begin promptly and without any prior reconnaissance or preparation. Stating what could not be said openly, the unit diarist bluntly condemned the decision, noting that, 'to undertake any operation except in the form of a "hit and run raid" on a small island without air support was the height of folly.'

CHAPTER 5

'Olforce'

LONG RANGE DESERT GROUP.

Operation Instruction No. 107

Secret.
Copy No.....
Date Oct 22 –24.

To:- J. Olivey. M.C.
OC, "OLFORCE"

1. Ref Map. ISOLA DI LEVITA 1:25000.
2. Composition of Force.

You will command a party of 4 Officers and 45 O.Rs. Your Force will be evenly divided into two sections. You will be OC SECTION ONE and Lt. Sutherland will be OC SECTION TWO. The whole will be known as "OLFORCE".

3. Task.

To liquidate any enemy Force that is on the Island of LEVITA.

4. Method.

I. Your party will be embarked by 2 M.Ls on the night of 23rd and should disembark at your destination on LEVITA. Island 2200 hours on the same night (see separate OLFORCE TIME programme.)

II. Sections are landed at different points on the Southern side of the Island and during the hours of darkness will be operating separately, linking together at dawn on the 24th.

III. The main objective is to obtain the high central ground overlooking PORTA LEVITA. If this is securely held it should be possible to deny the remaining portions of the Island to the enemy forces.

Baia del Fico, Levitha, landing place of Captain Olivey's Section 1. (Section 2, under Lieutenant Jack Sutherland, landed at Capo Tromba, on the south coast.)

Segnale: Location of Captain Olivey's Levitha headquarters (circled).

'P. J.', eldest and last surviving son of John Olivey, at Segnale in 2024. Much of the damage seen here occurred during the 'Brandenburg' operation on 18 October 1943 (the first floor of what was originally a two-storey structure has since collapsed).

Part of the battleground defended by Lieutenant Sutherland's Section 2, with Segnale and the Castello feature in the distance.

Memorial plaque placed at Levitha in September 2023.

Seen from a former German firing position, Point 320 in 2016. What was Battery Ciano is now a Greek naval base.

Evidence of close-quarter fighting in a tunnel below what was the battery command post.

Looking north-east from Point 320 towards Mount Vedetta.

Point 278. Grifo Bay is in dead ground, centre-left.

Alinda Bay. The distant central features are (left to right) Point 180 (Mount Appetici), Point 189 and Point 204 (Mount Meraviglia).

Alinda Bay (left) and Gurna Bay (right), with the *Fallschirmjäger* drop zone in-between. The feature centre-foreground is San Quirico.

L Cave.

Z Cave.

The 'trench' just below Battery Ciano, from where Lieutenant I. L. Brown and 13 Platoon of the King's Own mysteriously 'disappeared'.

Tail fin of a German 5 cm *Granatwerfer 36* below Mount Vedetta.

A British 3-inch mortar bomb in the area of Palma Bay, where a decisive action took place in view of those atop Clidi..

View from a former German machine-gun position, looking towards where Major Ernest Hole and several men of 4 Buffs were killed. In the distance: Clidi. The feature centre-right is Point 228.

Area held by C Company of the King's Own and the Italian barracks where Captain Olivey was taken prisoner.

Photomontage of *Pi-La-Boot H* sunk near Strongilo island on 12 November 1943.

IV. At 2000 hours the following day the 2 M.Ls return and either bring you any stores required or possibly an Italian Garrison to take over from you if it is known that you have liquidated the enemy opposition.

V. At the longest your party will be left on LEVITA for 48 hours.

5. Detail.

Section 1 and M.O attached.

a. Sections should be landed complete with all kit at map ref 725257 by 2200 hours on 23rd.
b. All stores for dumping are placed amongst the rocks.
c. Assault boats are hauled up and put in an inconspicuous position.
d. Whole party advances in battle formation and occupies M. VARDIA feature Map Ref 730259.
e. OC Section then proceeds to occupy the SEGNALE feature Map Ref 739259, where he will attempt to establish his HQ and site his Collins W/T and Medical Aid Post.
f. From here axis of advance should swing northwards towards the Western end of PAGLIA MUNDRA Map Ref 739265. This area if occupied by enemy should have been softened by fire from M.L. No one before shore party arrives there. Every effort should be made to occupy this area by dawn, on the 24th. At this time No. 2 Section will attempt to link up their most westerly detachment with No.1 Section to assist in the holding of the central high ground.
g. OC Section will have to decide if it is necessary to leave a rearguard occupying M. VARDIA, as he advances.
h. W/T communication between the two parties should be possible throughout and also back to the M.Ls whilst they are standing off the Islands (See separate W/T instructions)
j. After dawn the united parties will be used to the best advantage under command OC No. 1 Section.

Detail continued Section 2.

a. Section should be landed complete with all kit at Ref 733253 by 2200 hours A 23rd.

b. All stores for dumping will be placed in a hidden position in the rocks.
c. Assault boats to be hauled up and put in an inconspicuous position.
d. Whole party advances towards LA MADILLIAKA (Map Ref. 745263) Any light opposition encountered from area Mt. CALASURIA Map Ref. 760255 will not be allowed to divert the general direction of the advance.
e. A Section HQ will be established in the MADALLINA area and detachments will be sent off to try and clean up any enemy in the district marked CAMP (Map Ref 755265). This should be done between 2230 hours on the 23rd and dawn on the 24th.
f. At dawn Section 2 should try and link up with Section 1 whilst still retaining what commanding positions they have occupied during the night. The detachments sent down to the plain to mop up the CAMP area should have moved back to Section HQ near MADILLINA.
g. If possible a detachment should be placed on CASTELLO (Map Ref 742259). To avoid confusion with Section 1 this should not be done until daylight.

h)
j) See detail for Section 1.

SECTIONS 1 & 2.

In the case of the operation being unsuccessful both sections will attempt to work their way to the Western end of the Island and will hold this until nightfall when the arrival of the M.Ls will be reopened as from that time either by W/T or torch.

6. Information.

The I.O. will visit you on the 22nd and will provide you with all latest information and maps.

7. Additional Note.

Your party may obtain additional support by a bombardment by destroyer on the night of the 23rd. between the hours of 2200 and 2230 A but this cannot be relied upon.

Signed. Easonsmith. Major,
O.C L.R.D.G.

Field.
Oct 22 1943.

OLFORCE TIME PROGRAMME.

All Times are A Local time.

23rd Oct 43.	1830	hours.	2 M.Ls arrive wooden jetty ALINDA BAY.
	1930	"	Army party and stores embarked and sailed.
	2130	"	M.Ls reach their destination. No. 1 to Map Ref 725257 No. 2 to Map Ref 753253
	2200	"	Disembarkation completed M.L No. 1 moves to position off CLADARIA. or POTAMIA. Bays from which fire can be brought to bear on the Northern facing slopes of the feature PAGLIOMUNDRA. (Map Ref: 739260) and area. M.L No. 2 moves to VORINOPOLO Bay and brings fire to bear on Camp area (Map Ref: 7527)
	2230	"	M.Ls cease fire on their respective targets and cruise round to PUNTA FARO and from there back to their original positions. During the cruise they will open fire on the shores if there are any signs of enemy movement, paying particular attention to PONTA FARO and Mt. CALUSURIA.
	0300	"	Both M.Ls return to Base.
Oct 24th.	0200	"	Two M.Ls will be expected off Map Ref. 725257 Contact from shore will be made by W/T or torch.

<u>COMMENT.</u>

1. Four No. 18 W/T sets have been drawn one will be placed on each M.L and one will be carried by each of the Army Sections that is landed. (These sets are carried and need no fixing)

2. Army operators will be required to stay in the M.Ls to receive messages from the shore party.

3. If the Army party meets with no opposition; it will then be possible to notify the M.Ls and stop them from wasting ammunition.

4. The following visual signals will be flashed in Morse if necessary.
   M.M = Go to Alt.
   R.R = SEND A BOAT IN.
   S.S = DANGER KEEP OUT.

5. The British password will be AEGEAN.

6. The alternative R.V for pick up on the 24th is small bay on S.W (Map Ref 250709)

Field.
22 Oct 43.

(Sgd) J.R. EASONSMITH, Major,
OC., L.R.D.G.

ADMINISTRATIVE ORDER FOR "OLFORCE"

Major Alistar Guild.

You will be responsible for seeing that the following equipment etc is made available for OLFORCE and that the party is fully conversant in its use. The party must be fully prepared from midday the 23rd.

The layout of the force is as follows:-

SECTION ONE.
O.C (Capt. OLIVEY)
Lieut Kay.
W/T Op.
Med Ord.
2 Runners (1 of which is Reg Op)

(Det)	(Det)	(Det)	
N.C.O.	N.C.O.	N.C.O.	Att. to Sec. One.
&	&	&	Capt. LAWSON
5 O.Rs.	5 O.Rs.	4 O.Rs.	

SECTION TWO.
O.C (Lieut SUTHERLAND)
2 Runners (1 of which is Reg Sig)
1 Med Ord.

(Det)	(Det)	(Det)
N.C.O.	N.C.O	N.C.O
&	&	&
6 O.Rs.	4 O.Rs	6 O.Rs.

Arms. EACH DETACHMENT HAS – One Bren Gun with crew of two armed with revolvers and 2 Grenades.
12 Magazines per Bren Gun – 25 Rds per revolver.
One TSMG man with 200 Rds and 2 Grenades.
Remainder Riflemen with 200 Rds and 4 Grenades.

Section HQ Personnel to be armed at your discretion.
Each section had one 2" Mortar and 20 bombs.

Signalling.

W/T SECTION ONE. Has one Collins 18 M and 2 12v RAF Batteries and signal instruction.

Each Set. Has one 38 Walkie. Talkie sets and signal instruction to cover comn to its own M.L and to other Sect.
Each M.L must have provided one 38 Walkie - Talkie to communicate to the Section it drops.
You must obtain all instructions for men to use these and make sure that the RN end will work.

Visual.

Each Section must have 4 torches.
" " " " 4 Very pistols each with 6 of each colour cartridge.

Mens equipment to be Carried.

Food for three days. Water Sterilizing Tabs.
1 W/Bottle. First Field Dressing.

Dress.

Battle Dress.
Belt and Cross Straps.
W/Bottle Holder and Haversack.
Bren Gun, Pouches for B. Gunners and No. 2s.
Gas Capes if possible.

Additional per Section.

Stores to be prepared for quick and efficient dumping from Ship to Shore.

1 Stretcher.
1 Blanket per man.
1 Box Med Kit.
2 Spare Grenades per man in bulk.
2 Boxes 303 Ball.

6; 2 Gall water cans.

Boats.

1. 3 Assault to be allocated to each section.
2. Men to be trained in their use.
3. Every man to know his exact burden and position in the boat. Both practices on land and sea to be carried out.

MLs to be contacted and Section Commanders to know which boat they travel on.

Medical.

The doctor to be told to examine Medical Kits of both Orderlies and to attach himself to SECTION ONE as from midday the 23rd. Kit to be carried by himself and the Staff, must not hamper their easy movements. A reserve box weight up to 15 lbs may be dropped at the landing point of SECTION ONE if he desires but no guarantee can be given that he be able to move it from there or use it. Duration of his stay ashore is 48 hours, and it is fully realised that he cannot deal satisfactorily with major casualties.

Rehearsal.

When force is completely equipped, notify me as I wish to see a rehearsal on land of the men carrying their stores etc, as though from a landing boat to shore.

Field. (signed) Easonsmith. Major,
22 Oct 43. OC., L.R.D.G.

CHAPTER 6

The Battle of Levitha

The battle of Levitha hardly features in the annals of the Second World War, but it would have a lasting impact on the future organisation of the LRDG. When it was learned that Levitha was in Axis hands, the LRDG were ordered to retake the island. Olivey was required to report with most of his men, reinforced by a half-patrol, and a similar number of New Zealanders under Lieutenant Jack Sutherland – in all, some fifty personnel. Soldiers with little or no boating experience now had to hurriedly familiarise themselves with the unwieldy wood and canvas Goatley collapsible assault boat. To make matters worse, a hazardous delivery run on the deck of a destroyer had left them damaged by shrapnel. Sea trials had to be interrupted when a tear or hole was noticed, whereupon the boat was hauled on to dry land in order to carry out essential repairs.

Among those having to cope with the unenviable task was Trooper Ron Hill:

'We sat on a wall for a "drag and a spit", tired, getting hungry and wet through when along the road, in a cloud of dust, bowled a jeep, laden with brass hats, naturally inspiring the usual ribald comments from us, the rude soldiery. In a few moments the jeep returned, fast, in reverse and out poured a choleric, red-faced Brigadier [Brittorous], with adjutant. Slaying the unfortunate sergeant in charge he had us off the wall in a trice and called to attention: he wanted to know if we ever saluted our officers, metaphorically pointing to his red tabs. (He'd have burst a blood vessel if we'd said "No, only first thing in the morning"). So he dressed us down, good and proper, ending with the words, ominous

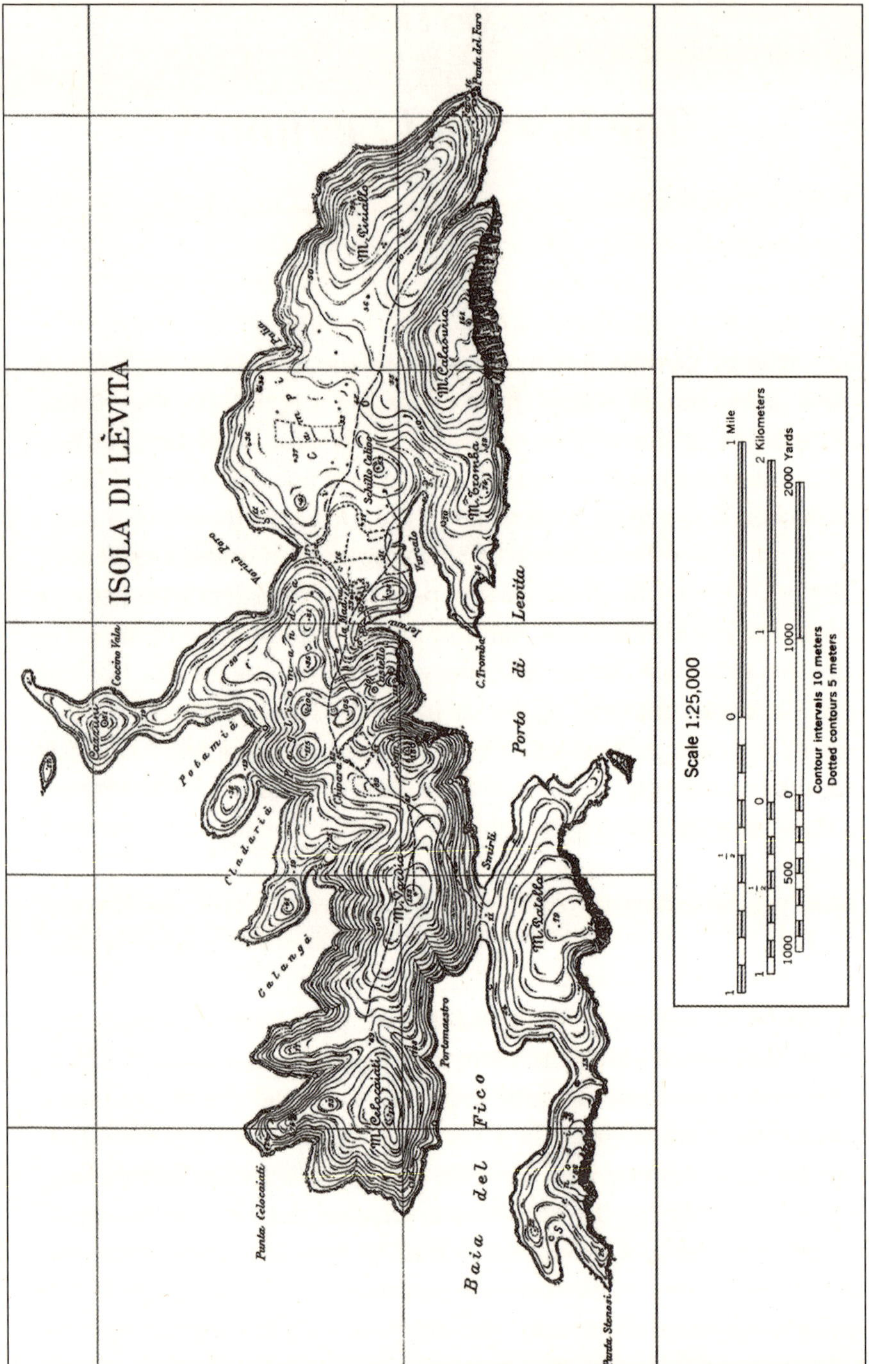

Map 4. Levitha

and prophetic, "So you think yourselves tough, do you? I'll bloody well give you something to be tough about."'

The 'sergeant' concerned was Bradfield. As Olivey recalled:

> We spent the morning practicing rowing or paddling flat bottomed landing boats which held about eight men and their kits. We drew rations for three days and an extra Bren gun and 2" mortar, an infantry W/T set and a set for transmitting for distances. I received my orders next day at noon – we were to go to Levitha in two M.L.s, Jack in one, I in the other. We would land on opposite ends of the island. The number of the enemy was said to be approximately fifty. We would land and occupy the high ground in the centre of the island. We should be reinforced after forty-eight hours. Thomas fell foul of the Brigadier through not saluting. He was told he had a good moustache, but not as good as the Brigadier's and what's more, he would salute. The Brigadier would make him tough if that's what he thought he was!
>
> We set off that evening in our respective M.L.s. I had with me Francis K. [sic: Lieutenant John Kay] who had been given to me at the last moment in place of Sergeant Jenk [Sydney Jenkinson], who had sore feet.

Section 1 had embarked on ML 836 commanded by Lieutenant Albert E. Clark, RNVR; Section 2 was on board ML 579 commanded by Lieutenant James Bain, RNVR.

> Everything went according to plan as far as the Navy was concerned. We landed safely and without opposition, hid our boats and blankets and spare kit. I sent one patrol on in front to the right and one to the left and kept one to carry the wireless gear and equipment.

Ron Hill described the landing of Section 2:

'Embarking into the tossing and pitching folboats [sic], down the scramble mats from the ML, in pitch darkness, was almost suicidal, particularly when the NZ sergeant [New Zealander, Edwin J. Dobson] slipped when lowering himself into the boat and fell head first almost capsizing it, water pouring over the free board. For one awful moment I had visions of going to the bottom of the Aegean, laden down as I was with a Tommy gun and spare magazines, two pouches of hand grenades, to say nothing of my heavy German rock-climbing boots. Somehow, we staggered ashore through the surf and heavy swell, dragged the folboat into hiding among the rocks, scaled the cliffs and our invasion was on. In the meanwhile, the ML had landed the other party and begun to give "covering" fire by shelling the enemy HQ, which succeeded only in waking up the enemy to the realisation that something was afoot. Thereafter, Germans seemed to materialise from nowhere all over the island.'

Olivey's Section 1 initially had a much easier time after having come ashore inside a comparatively sheltered bay:

> We climbed a steep hill and all met again on the top. I changed the patrols around and we proceeded. This time I moved in front. Our objective was the fort on top of a hill. We moved slowly up to this hill with the moon setting just behind it. It was an excellent time to approach and I pushed on. The fort had a wire fence around it with a machine gun pointing out our way.

The 'fort', situated centrally on high ground (Segnale), was the same two-storey Italian structure targeted by Arados during the recent 'Brandenburg' operation. Nearby was a smaller outhouse. A number of defence works surrounded the buildings.

> I halted the force outside the fence and went forward with three men. We crept up to the machine gun and found it was not manned. All the way up I had thought I saw people moving in the shadows. We split up and met on the other side of the fort. There was no sign of life – the fort was unoccupied. We occupied it. Jack was having a battle. We could hear shots were being exchanged on his end of the island, but so far it seemed the enemy were not

aware of our presence. I gave the troops an easy and we rested for an hour. Our second objective was two hills to the north and these I was to occupy at daylight where I should meet Jack. As he was obviously in difficulties and my presence seemed unknown, I decided to take these two hills just before dawn. Thomas and a British corporal were to go with their patrols and take these hills. They set off about an hour before dawn. I and a small force remained at the fort. At dawn, I heard firing north-west of the fort and thought that one of our patrols had run into Jack's patrol. Shortly afterwards, however, mortar fire opened up on this patrol and it was obviously Jerry. One enemy aircraft passed overhead with signals exchanged.

I heard one of the men shouting in the valley below and almost immediately, machine-gun fire from the enemy swept that area. There was then silence. Daylight was just coming on and we could now see the enemy position quite clearly. I had placed the patrol remaining on the fort so that all trenches were occupied and the W/T set was in a hole behind the fort, well under cover. Just before sunrise about twelve Germans appeared on their hill, and with them a soldier in British uniform who commenced signalling in semaphore. At first his signals were readable but shortly [afterwards] they got very erratic and quite unreadable.

Having briefly considered, then promptly rejecting, the possibility that the Germans were offering to surrender, Olivey concluded that they must instead be requesting his surrender.

My reply to his signals was a few rifle shots in the direction and he and his prisoner scattered to their trenches.

At this moment the Rhodesian patrol returned and with them supporting Thomas, who had been badly wounded in the arm. He was handed over to the doctor who had made his aid post in a cement gun emplacement. It seems that this patrol had either lost their way or tried too much, for they had approached the enemy position instead of the hills they were to have occupied and the enemy had opened up on them on a pathway. They had been too

> much bunched as will often happen the first time under fire and this had cost them Thomas's wound.
>
> Kevan and his No. 2 on the gun had been captured. They were to give covering fire to the withdrawing party, though no shot was fired and it then became obvious that it was Kevan who had been signalling from the hill top. We did not see his No. 2, van Heerden, but Kevan appeared and reappeared, dodging from trench to trench all day.

Nearly sixty years later, Kevan described a different version of events. He recalled that his three-man reconnaissance patrol had been tasked before dawn to cross a nearby valley and ascend the facing slope.

'This we did, widely spaced, and all seemed to be quiet and peaceful until, as we neared the summit, (I presume "we" because I was out of contact with the other two) a storm of bullets rattled round the rocks beside me. I dived for cover behind one of the larger rocks and returned fire into the darkness with my tommy-gun, otherwise I kept my head down. The enemy was only a few yards above me. At daybreak I watched helplessly as Stukas attacked the patrol on the hillside opposite. […]

'At about 0830 I heard a sound nearby and turning my well-kept-down head I was dismayed to see a German soldier a few feet away pointing a heavy machine gun at me. The decision was quickly made – dead hero or live prisoner – so I threw my weapons and rocksack [sic] down the hill and cautiously made my way up to the German position as directed. I should say that while I was behind my rock I was exposed to "friendly fire" from our people opposite. That I was not hit was probably luck rather than judgement.'

Kevan was escorted to an inlet on the northern side of the island and later that morning flown in an Arado to the mainland. 'We took off and, before heading for Greece, made a couple of strafing passes over my patrol which was unpleasant.'

As for Olivey and his men still atop Segnale:

We now settled down to exchanging rifle and machine-gun fire. I borrowed someone's rifle, and having spotted someone on top of their first hill observing through glasses, I took a shot at him. I had the satisfaction of seeing him fall to the ground, and at the time, I thought he was hit, but it is impossible to say. We brought machine-gun fire on anyone presenting a good enough target and sniped them with rifles. The two positions were just too far apart to allow accurate fire and I had 600 yards on my sights.

I set two men to prepare breakfast and signalled the position of things to H.Q. Jack was having a great battle in his area and things were warming up with us as they had brought a mortar to fire on our positions and their ranging was good, one bomb dropping on the top of our trench spattered us with rock but otherwise did no damage.

Just before breakfast, a seaplane suddenly started up from below our position and set straight out to sea, and flew away for Kos. The plane returned shortly afterwards and proceeded into its original position. I opened up from my height and some NZ opened up at the same time from the other side of the bay. The pilot swung his plane round with one float well under the water. He then taxied out to sea, took a very long run, eventually getting into the air, only to take an immediate crash-landing into the sea. We had shot down one plane.

This cheered everyone considerably and also to know that Jack was making headway. I had a W/T set to communicate with him but I could never get any reply to my signals, and concluded he was too hard pressed. We had found difficulty in carrying all our gear, so he had no doubt found the same, with a battle to fight on top of it. The other patrol returned at this stage, and having had breakfast, I sent two patrols out to the left, for I feared the Germans might try to work round and we had observed several of them withdrawing to the camp at the rear.

The 'camp' referred to by Olivey and in LRDG operation reports was an area in north Levitha, shown on Italian maps as *i Campi* (the fields).

These two patrols had difficulty in getting forward as machine-gun fire was keeping them down and mortar bombs came over as soon as they were in range. I sent two men of the patrol with me back for our 2" mortar and bombs and as much ammo as they could carry. The fight still [sic: then?] became one of exchanging shots and I tried to persuade the two patrols on the left to get forward. We are not a trained infantry unit, however, and this was obviously an infantry job, so we contented ourselves with occupying the high ground across to the left. I was, therefore, rather out of touch with these two patrols, and Jack seemed to have withdrawn to the right. So things remained for some time, with mortar and rifle fire interruptions.

About noon, the two men returned with mortar bombs and ammunition and brought with them three prisoners they had picked up in a ditch near our landing spot. We bundled these into the fort and tried to question them. I sent for our German speaker but he never appeared and I had to rely on my own small knowledge of German.

The German-speaker was probably Gunner Herbert Federmann, a Czechoslovakian Jew who had emigrated to Palestine shortly before the war. He was killed on Levitha.

It seemed that these three Germans, one of whom was an under-sergeant [*Unterfeldwebel*], had been in charge of a small cottage just above our landing spot. They had obviously been asleep when we landed. They had left their cottage and were coming up the path we had already taken when they saw our two men behind them with the ammunition. They had thought they were cut off from their own side and had got into the ditch to hide when the two Rhodesians had come upon them. I was unable to find out from them the strength of the garrison against us, more especially as at that moment the Luftwaffe decided to attack and circled our fort, machine-gunning the walls and dropping a number of bombs in the area. The Germans do not like bombing and seem to consider their own pilots as experts at dropping them in the right place. These three sat under the table shivering for all they were fit and bemoaning their fate that they should be inside the fort which they were certain would be flattened.

It was impossible to obtain any sense from them at all. One of the Rhodesians, who had brought them up, I put as guard over them, gave them some water, some wood and a mess tin, with instructions to cook up some tea and open a tin of milk and 'bully' [corned beef], ready for lunch later on, when the bombing was over. I then went back to my trench. From this time on, I spent in various positions around the fort, having shots at the Germans over on their hill. I moved about as much as possible to give the impression that there were a number of men in the fort all firing.

The doctor had, I noticed, moved his patient out of the fort area to some broken country south-west of the fort. Here, he was far better off as the bombing would not disturb his patient who had lost a lot of blood, but was doing well.

Signals had got through to H.Q. and put [sic: sent?] my first message but could still not get Jack. I prepared another message, giving the latest results, but when I went to hand it to them, found the set but no signallers. John Kay was over in the trench to the left of our front with one man and so I, with R. [Gunner Jacobus F. 'Jack' Rupping], another Rhodesian, took up a position on the right. The Germans signal to their aircraft on occasions like this with red smoke bombs from their mortars and they were signalling them to leave our troop and attack the NZs. I had hoped that our patrol on the left would take advantage of this and try to get forward. Things quietened down in our area so much so that sitting in my trench I could hear sheep grazing down the valley. I thought what a nice homely sound the sheep bells had and noticed that they were slowly working their way up the hill towards us.

In his narrative, Olivey makes frequent mention of sheep, which, together with goats, roam freely on both Levitha and Leros. These animals were to make a lasting impression, as will be seen.

I continued to have occasional shots at the enemy and at the aircraft when they came over. The trench I was in was L-shaped so that it was easy to dodge approaching planes, who still brought their machine guns to fire on us when passing over. There were about fifteen planes over the island most of the time. The seaplanes would touch down in a position out of range to us, and, no doubt, out of view to Jack, and close to the enemy camp. The Stukas would need to return to Kos and there, collect more bombs, ammo and petrol. As the afternoon wore on, so the Stukas got less, though there were still six or seven seaplanes over us. These were, no doubt, able to pick up supplies where they touched down. Jack was getting particular blazes knocked out of his force at this time. They, according to the fire, seemed to have been beaten back to their starting point and bombs and mortars were constantly in their area. There was nothing I could do about it except wait for night when we could take the Germans on on even terms, when we knew their air force would be unable to support them.

The sheep grazed right up to the left side of the fort and then seemed to go back again. There was quite a lull in the battle around about 1600 hours.

Half an hour later I heard John Kay call my name. I let him shout. I thought, "He knows where I am, why can't he come over?" Later, thinking it might be a message or himself hurt, I went back to the fort. I found John standing between two Germans with steel helmets on. I thought they were two of our original three at first, until I noticed that they had machine guns. I quickly pulled my revolver – I had left my rifle in the trench – at the same moment John Kay noticed me and shouted, "I'm in the bag, so are you and the whole show is over." I shouted back, "Like hell, I am", fired a couple of shots to make the Jerries think and ran with their bullets after me. Fortunately, they were not very good shots. I ran back to the trench, told Rupping to get a move on and follow me. He passed up the rifles and I moved on forward. I had not noticed before a cut in the wire straight in front of me and we went through this. It led left down a path to the German fort or right over a

> sheer drop of 15–20 feet. Without considering, I chose the 15-foot drop and jumped in less time than it takes to write. Rupping threw down the rifles to me, my binoculars and map case which he had thoughtfully picked up.

The 'German fort' is thought to refer to a sizeable ancient ruin 475 yards north-east of Segnale.

> The Germans were standing about on the fort opposite and I thought they must have seen us, right on the skyline as were. We were a few feet only to the right where a ledge overhung a few green bushes in the rocks. Here we dived in and remained perfectly still. Perhaps the Germans opposite were facing the other way. In any case, they made no sign of having seen us and all depended on our remaining still. It was not a very comfortable position and we had an hour and a half to pass before dark. The Germans above started by throwing grenades in our trench. The explosions above us made us glad we had not stayed there. The first two or three must have been bad shots as they had several. Next, we heard the Jerry come up and shout to us in the trench. Next, he came through the fence, and shouting in German, "Ich sehe Sie! Kommen Sie her!" [I can see you! Come here!], fired a few rifle shots down the hillside. The shots chiefly went down the valley, though one or two passed overhead. He obviously hadn't the faintest idea where we were, although shouting he could see us. I pulled the pin of a grenade ready to throw at him should he attempt the jump we had just done, or come round the path – which would lead him, most likely, away from us. He did neither, and on receiving a signal from the other fort, gave us up for the time.
>
> Our immediate danger was over, though we still could not move as the Germans were still watching from the other fort. Fortunately, the sun was in their eyes, and, as it dropped, I could see the shadow creeping up their hill. I waited until it was near the top and then told Rupping we might move our very cramped limbs. Just after this was our most dangerous light as, with no sun in their eyes, we could be easily seen.

Nearly all of Olivey's section would fall into captivity. Gunner J. D. (Jim) Patch returned to Segnale with his patrol, little realising that Olivey had been forced to evacuate the position:

'As we approached our H.Q. at about 4.30 pm, we observed some of our own men walking freely about round the outside wall of the house and therefore approached without caution. As we drew near, however, we found ourselves covered by two Spandau MGs [machine guns] manned by Germans who had been concealed behind a low wall. A German then came out of the building and called upon us to surrender and at the same time the rest of the enemy party numbering about fifteen men appeared from their hiding places. The men from our own party who we had seen near the building were Lieutenant Kay and 3 or 4 Rhodesians who were already prisoners when we saw them. They informed me that [Lance Corporal J. E.] Harris' patrol had all been made prisoners. I was then marched down to the German H.Q. where Harris and his patrol were being held. This H.Q. was in a small group of stone houses situated in the centre of the island. Harris told me that his patrol had been attacked simultaneously from two sides by two enemy patrols each of which outnumbered his own. In the skirmish that followed Gunner [Herbert] Federmann had been killed before the patrol was forced to surrender. Private [David] Gunn, however, did not surrender but lay low and made his escape. The Germans were very friendly towards us, and their commander, a lieutenant, saluted us formally and told us that his sergeant had reported to him that we were "good soldiers".'

For the time being, Olivey and Rupping remained in hiding, but their situation had become extremely precarious.

> We now saw our own troops filing down the path to the German fort. There seemed to be no guard over them, though Germans were still looking for our men on the hills to the left and sometimes throwing grenades or firing into bushes.
>
> We were able to recognise several of our men and it seemed that most of the patrols were prisoners. Firing had slackened in Jack's quarter, and at dark completely stopped.

Ron Hill described the surrender of most of Section 2 (four men would evade capture for several days before giving themselves up):

'The mortaring had now stopped but the enemy was now close enough to subject the area to fire from rifle grenades. It was now somewhere around six o'clock. Captain Sutherland then said he would surrender to save further bloodshed as no useful purpose could be served by holding on. From the position of the enemy at this time he concluded the boats had already been captured. This was confirmed later by the NZ sergeant who attempted to reach them and was brought in the next day by the Germans. Our ammunition had also been expended and we were by this time using captured arms. By the time Captain Sutherland made this decision it was too late for any one in our party to take evasive action especially as our position was in full view of the enemy prisoners. Captain Sutherland thereupon sent out a German prisoner to inform the attackers and displayed a white flag. Whilst this was going on I threw what arms I could including the captured machine gun and mortar over the cliffs into the sea. The German prisoners we had taken earlier in the day then took over and we were taken to the German H.Q. where we met most of Captain Olivey's party.'

For Olivey and Rupping, however, surrender was never an option.

> At dark, we collected our rifles, which we had pushed into the bushes, our other kit, and moved off slowly round the hill. One always seems to make a tremendous noise at night and our clinker boots seemed to resound on every rock on the hill. I wondered if we should find the doctor or if he had been captured.
>
> I knew that from my signal they would send an M.L. to collect the wounded man, so we made for the R.V., returning the same way as we had come up, arriving there at about 2000 hours. We found a little water in one of the tins, which was most welcome. We launched one of our boats, not without difficulty, as it is a four-man load at least, and rowed out in the bay a little way, putting into the west side where it was dark and hauled our boat onto the rocks and proceeded to wait for the expected M.L. It

was very cold. Our feet had got wet launching and paddling our boat and I found a few dried peaches in my pouches, which we ate. We did not like to eat them all in case the M.L. did not arrive. We might have to wait the whole of the next day. I must have fallen asleep and I woke up stiff and cold but I thought I heard the M.L., but no, it was Rupping snoring! At about 2300 hours, the M.L. was heard creeping into the bay. These boats seem to make a tremendous noise when you are in them, but were only just audible when one is listening for them. We quickly launched our boat and paddled for all we were fit for the boat. I was frightened that receiving no signal from us they would move out again. We had, for this reason, put ourselves on the seaward side of the M.L. We now saw a fire burning on the shore and at the same time a voice called us from the opposite shore. The M.L. asked for the password, which we gave. Soon, we were in conversation with the M.L. commander and Jake, who had come out with it. The fire had been started by the doctor, so we were told by the man on the shore, so we took our boat back there. Here, we found Dick with his medical orderly and wounded man, also a signaller and another Rhodesian. We took the doctor and Thomas with the medical orderly and sent the others round the shore where we would pick them up. Thomas had revived wonderfully and was able, with a little help, to climb up the scrambling ropes onto the M.L. His one arm was badly damaged and he had wounds in his side. He had given very little trouble so Dick said and had done wonderfully, after recovering from the first shock, which everyone who is wounded seems to get. We went back to pick up the other two on the shore. They pulled our legs at having paddled so fast after the M.L. that it looked as though we had put engines in our canoe.

We talked over what had happened. Dick had seen John Kay calling everyone in after he was captured. He seemed rather to have lost his head and given several people over to the enemy. Dick had also [---] a lot of Anglo-German friendship and exchanged cigarettes when our men were captured. One man was heard to say, "I your prisoner, you give me cigarettes, now I give you cigarettes."

No doubt, our previous prisoners! The Rhodesian I had left in charge of them seemed to me to be too kindly disposed towards his prisoners and kept on leaving his automatic pistol lying about where they could easily have snatched it up. Only afterwards did I discover that, in any case, this pistol could not fire! The signaller and the other Rhodesian had got away by being out of the fort when the Germans entered it. They had remained hidden in the bush until dark and had then moved back. They had seen several chaps give themselves up on the order that all was over, thinking no doubt, that we had won the day. It all seemed so sudden that it might have deceived either side. The Germans had seemed suddenly to rise out of the ground behind us and I thought that they must have worked their way round our left flank, but they must have moved very quickly as it was a long way round the coast and it was only afterwards that, I think, I discovered what really happened.

The M.L. cruised close to the shore in the hope that we might pick up some of Jack's party in boats. No sign of them was to be seen, however, although we put right into their landing spot. As the M.L. had to get under camouflage before daylight, we had to return to Leros and arrived there at about 0400 hours. The M.L. commander gave us a drink on board, also some hot tea and soup, which was more than welcome. Sergeant Jenk had some stew for us at camp and we slept till daybreak.

The majority of 'Olforce' would spend the rest of the war in captivity. Notable exceptions were Ron Hill and Jim Patch, who joined Yugoslav *Četnici* after escaping from a train while en route to Germany. Gunner Herbert Federmann was dead. Nobody could say what happened to Troopers John T. Bowler and Douglas A. Davison, who remain missing to this day. Neither of the two seriously wounded on 24 October survived: Trooper Hector L. Mallett died the next day and Trooper Archibald J. Penhall followed, soon after being evacuated to the mainland. Sergeant Dobson would die in captivity in the last weeks of the war. It was the worst single disaster to have befallen the force. Only Olivey,

Rupping, 'Doc' Lawson, medical orderly Lance Corporal Vincent 'Spud' Murphy, the wounded Bradfield and two more ORs evaded capture to be evacuated by motor launch.

The LRDG would never be the same after the disaster of Levitha, which would lead to the New Zealand government withdrawing its countrymen from LRDG service. The New Zealand Squadron was disbanded two months later, on 31 December 1943.

CHAPTER 7

Lull Before the Storm

Jake woke me up early as we had to go and report to the C.O. at H.Q. I spent the morning making out a report with Dick C. [Captain Cecil H. B. 'Dick' Croucher] and later in the day a Brigadier from M.E. questioned me about things. It was quite obvious that without our own air cover our own troops could do nothing, as their Luftwaffe just kept our heads down while their ground troops moved about as they pleased. "This is merely what will happen here," said our C.O. "No," replied the Brigadier, "the navy and the air force can and will play."

I had asked permission to go back that night with the M.L. in the hope that some of my force might still make the R.V. So, I went and had a sleep in Dick Croucher's bed and felt refreshed again by 1500 hours. I went down to the hospital to see Thomas but he had been operated on that afternoon and had not come out of the anaesthetic. I collected my kit from camp and went to draw a spare pair of trousers from Q. Tim H., our signal officer, was leaving for Cairo that night, so I took the chance to write him out a cable to send to you [Micky], with all my love, and gave him a quid to pay expenses. It would cost him 17/6 [17 shillings and 6 pence]. I didn't work the 3/- number sentences which seldom arrive in South Africa, so I had found. There was quite a party going on in Q stores. Someone had a bottle of whisky and a couple of bottles of German wine were being drunk. I believe it was David's birthday. In any case, it was quite jolly and I left feeling confident that I should bring back a number of chaps. Alister [sic] G. and I left together. He was coming with me. We arrived at the quay, but after waiting for an hour, still no M.L. turned up. We sent our driver

> back to Navy House to ask the reason. They came rushing down and took us to another part of the harbour. There had been some mistake and no boat was laid on, but one quickly was and we found ourselves travelling in Jack's M.L. of the night before.

The Brigadier introduced to Olivey was George M. O. Davy, Director of Military Operations at General Headquarters, Middle East; Tim H. was Major Geoffrey B. 'Tim' Heywood; Alister G. was Major Alastair I. Guild, OC A Squadron. Navy House was the name given by the British to a requisitioned building inland of Alinda Bay, on the road to Parteni.

> We arrived on the R.V. at about midnight and I asked for two hours on shore. This was allowed and I put to shore on one side of our R.V. I walked right up the path again which we had first taken, first making sure that our hidden boats and blankets had not been touched, so the enemy didn't know where we had landed. There was no sign of any of our men and I went so far as to shout down into the bay on the other side before returning, but only sheep could be heard. These sheep were grazing down the hill towards me. After making a circle round to the right, I signalled for the boat just two hours from the time I went ashore. This other coast was rather rough for the small boat, so I had to bring it a bit farther back. The sheep seemed to be very close. I asked permission to stay on the island to have a good look by daylight and I could be picked up next night, but Alastair Guild would not allow this, as he had orders that no more men were to be lost on this exploit. So, we crossed round close to the shore and shelled their fort on the hill in the hope of causing some trouble, but I doubt very much if it had any effect on the enemy.

Unbeknown to Olivey, four LRDG who had evaded capture remained in hiding on Levitha. Eventually, they had no choice but to give themselves up, joining those who were already prisoners of war. The ML was to have returned to Levitha again that night, but later in the day was sunk at Arki by Ju 88s. Lieutenant James Bain, Sub-

Lieutenant John M. Cooke and Able Seaman Francis A. Sandison were killed. Two were seriously wounded: Able Seaman Augustus W. Smith died in hospital at Leros two days later; Able Seaman Albert Dunscombe survived.

> Our lookout on Leros had reported a small steamship with aircover which had visited the island and returned to C. during the day. Also, the previous night, a large flying-boat had landed and made for Greece shortly after dark, so our chaps had most likely all been taken off. Thinking over this exploit afterwards, I cannot see how we had hoped to hold this island or what value it could be to us. There was hardly a level spot on the place and it seems we have no seaplanes to act as fighters in any case, so we had lost forty-three of the best chaps for nothing, as far as could be seen.

German forces tasked with holding Levitha were justifiably concerned following their encounter with the LRDG, so much so, that the officer commanding, Leutnant Dietzsch, had demanded they be reinforced with another platoon, 'Otherwise the island will be handed over.' Within days, he and his men were relieved by troops of 1./1.Rgt. 'Brandenburg'.

> I had a good sleep on the way back in a bunk and also a few hours on arrival on shore. Had a bath in an old rain tub and a shave and after a day's rest, felt much better. Next day I went to see Thomas, but found that he had been taken back to the mainland the night before. I had a day's rest under the olive trees in what had almost become a rest camp. Charlie S. [Captain Saxton] had just returned from a watch of shipping on an island near Greece and was supposed to be going back to the mainland with his men. Alan Redfern had just returned from his watch on Rhodes and was now Major and my Squadron Commander, David having moved to 2 i/c Unit and Jake to C.O., the C.O. taking up a staff appointment with R.F. [Raiding Forces]. I was glad to see Alan and to find him happy in his new appointment, which should have been mine had I had a bent that way.

Redfern had been unable to infiltrate Rhodes and instead had undergone an eventful time on Simi, before returning to Leros on 22 October. He was appointed B Squadron commander the next day, whereupon Olivey relinquished his position as 2 i/c B Squadron and took over Redfern's S1 Patrol. The LRDG War Diary records that as such Olivey 'could exercise his operational talent to a much greater degree than had been possible in his previous role'. Years later, Olivey disclosed to 'Stuka' Stokes: 'Prendergast asked me if I'd make a good Squadron Commander and I told him I'd make a bloody awful one and he said well they thought so too … I have never been so glad in my life as when I was demoted or at least not promoted …'

> It was said that David would be going back to Cairo very shortly and it was hoped we should all in our Unit get back there very shortly. Jake would make an excellent C.O., popular, knowing his job and his men, and everyone anxious to serve him.
>
> I was returned to my post on the hill and found Sergeant C. P. [Lorenzo 'Cito' Calder Potts] and an almost new lot of chaps there. The signallers were the same, however, and my Ox was still faithfully carrying on. I had now Alan Redfern's patrol to command. I requisitioned and obtained a bale of sandbags, as I had ideas that our fort would need to be strengthened against much air attack as we had had recently. There was still a skeleton B. Squadron in the broken country to the west, but four of their number joined me and Lance Corporal Randel [sic: R. O. 'Mick' Rundle] was in charge of this attachment.
>
> I started by digging a trench round the old No. 1 gun and on the edge of the gun emplacement, as from here I could observe all below the hill and used parts of the old gun as cover from the air, strengthening it with sandbags and making this position strong, as a lookout post. I dug a shallow trench leading back to the fort and behind the old gun. This took several days to dig and gave me something to do in the morning by way of exercise. I ordered the men to make themselves dugouts, and make themselves comfortable at the same time against the coming rains.

Until now, those at Battery Ciano had made do with rudimentary shelter, but with the ongoing air attacks, expected German invasion and approaching winter, better defensive structures were considered necessary. Even so, Olivey was concerned whether the new positions would be able to withstand heavy fire.

> I made a strong square emplacement behind No. 2 gun, which would protect our rear and be a useful spot for wounded or suchlike purposes. This, I built up with sandbags one and a half [feet] thick and about 4 foot square and ordered Sergeant Calder Potts to occupy with Bennett [Rifleman Andrew F. Bennett] and their Bren. I now had three Brens on the fort and had collected a number of boxes of grenades.
>
> We were continuously getting warning from M.E. or other sources that the proposed invasion was to take place. Stanley Eastwood had landed on Calino and not been heard of since, but we now got a message that three men were there, and would we collect them?

In fact, Lieutenant Eastwood was a prisoner of war, though not for long. When contact had been lost with his patrol, New Zealander Sergeant Robert D. Tant was tasked with landing on Kalymnos to discover the reason. He, too, was captured, joining Eastwood and three of his four men. All would escape soon afterwards, after being taken to Kos for transportation to the mainland. Tant and one man returned to Leros on 5 November, to be followed that night by the only patrol member to have evaded capture. Eastwood, together with two of his men, succeeded in reaching neutral Turkey.

> Our own forces on the island were being reinforced almost each night and it was now known we had at least three infantry battalions on the island, also some more guns and gunners. My own gunners had been taken away for other duties and I had trained a team to be in charge of blowing the gun when necessary. Alan used to come up and spend odd evenings with me and we would talk of the possibility of invasion. I was almost certain that

no invasion would take place, though this feeling in no way made us slacken our lookout. We kept a daily log and recorded every small happening that we noticed and filled sheets of paper with ships' movements.

Our Brigadier was changed at the time and we were now under a most energetic man from Cairo, who visited all our posts and asked numerous questions. Our previous Brigadier had rather dug himself in a hole where he stayed all day!

Major-General H. R. Hall and Brigadier R. A. G. 'Dolly' Tilney had arrived on Leros on 5 November, following which, Headquarters Aegean assumed control of operations. Hall chose to locate his headquarters on Samos and departed on 11 November, leaving on Leros, Tilney, who replaced recently promoted (soon to be demoted) Major-General Brittorous as Fortress Commander. Acting on instructions of Major-General Hall, Tilney ordered a drastic reorganisation of the established defence plan.

The basic strategy was to deny the beaches to the enemy. The island was divided into three sectors, with troops deployed on a dangerously wide front, thereby aggravating the already poor line of communications. An under-strength 4th Battalion The Royal East Kent Regiment (The Buffs) was deployed in the north, the Faughs (with B Company of 2nd Battalion The Queen's Own Royal West Kent Regiment) in the centre, and most of 1st Battalion The King's Own Royal Regiment (Lancaster) in the south. Each battalion, with one company held as local reserve, was sited to cover potential landing places on the coast. Units also had to be ready to move into any sector and under the authority of the area commander. Fortress reserve (C Company of the King's Own) was held near San Quaranta, south of Clidi, with the primary task of counter-attacking paratroopers who might be dropped in the north sector. All British transport – about ten jeeps – was allotted to the company each evening until 'stand down' the following morning. Medium machine guns were sited to sweep likely landing areas; four 25-pounders were placed centrally on a feature in the Blacutera area (between San Giovanni and Meraviglia), and 2-pounder antitank guns and 40mm Bofors were installed at strategic points in and around the centre of the island. The uncertain loyalty and fighting quality of the Italians led to their being dispersed throughout the island. When the battle began, they were destined to play a comparatively minor role.

Allied forces on Leros would eventually number approximately 3,350 mainly British army personnel, together with an estimated 5,000–6,000 Italians, most, but not all of them, military.

> The [Royal Artillery] gunners had a practice shoot and came up to the fort to observe their fire. They were so struck with the possibilities of Pt. 320 that they posted a Lieutenant P. [Harold Price] to live with me and he took up residence with his two signallers. He made his O.P. in my trench, although I suggested that he made himself a position – it did not seem to occur to him that I might need this spot I had made for myself. There were plenty of other possible positions which, with a little improvement, could be made as good. His telephone line was brought into this trench, and, generally, he took the position over. The telephone was not a great success as, to get to his guns, he had to pass through an exchange, which would continuously be cutting him off. His W/T set, however, gave him communication with the guns, though he had trouble in getting a set which would work to his satisfaction.
>
> One morning, our lookout called me as to the west appeared a convoy of enemy shipping. At first, we counted eight. This number afterwards increased to fourteen and nineteen in another convoy farther behind. All these ships which, as they got closer, we were able to see consisted of three or four destroyers, six or seven landing craft and the remainder 'caiques' or Greek sailing boats with auxiliary engines, were heading for C. They had sufficient air cover to keep off [---] or any naval craft, but surely now was the time for our bombers from Cyprus to put in an attack.

This, Generalleutnant Müller's invasion fleet, continued practically unhindered and assembled at Kos and Kalymnos. There was very little those on Leros could do, except watch and wait.

They kept out of range of any of our guns, though the fort of San Giorgio [gun battery at Scumbarda] did attempt a few rounds in their direction, at which the German destroyers tried to disperse the convoy a bit and get them farther off the coast. It was the talk of the island for the next day or two.

The air attacks had grown in intensity and we had now resorted to firing back at them with Bren gun fire. It seemed that we and H.Q. were a favoured target and many attacks were launched at us. Often, we thought the bombing was very bad as the bombs would drop some distance from the fort and in the ground to the east, where no troops were posted and where there was no military objective. Our Scotti had done good work and had put in some very good shooting at these enemy aircraft. Bombs continually dropped close, but none now damaged our guns. They were dropping a number of these bombs which look like rugby footballs and are about 3 feet wide and 5 feet long. They make a tremendous explosion and dust, but seem otherwise useless. The German is a great believer in noise, however. It was always our hope to hit one of these bombs as it left the plane. The rock on the fort is very much like the rock of Malta, in that it does not splinter when hit, but seems to crumble under the explosion of bombs and goes to powder. These football bombs just made dust, therefore, and did no harm. I should not have liked to have one in my trench, however, which was perhaps the idea of them, to blow down the walls of our trenches, which, after all, were only piled up stone.

It was now almost full moon and I had always maintained that the enemy would attack at full moon, if at all, as then our Navy could not support us as they could on dark nights.

We received a message that our spies in Athens had reported that a parachute battalion had arrived in that city. Tonight was surely 'the night'. The bombing was very heavy all day and in the evening six Ju 88s came right over the fort, diving but not bombing. They then made a figure of eight turn to the east and dived and bombed right across the centre of the island. I watched them with interest, and as they dived, I remarked to Lieutenant Price, "There are the parachutists of tomorrow. They are now taking a look at their landing spot." I felt convinced that an attack was now coming that night. I took the precaution of seeing that all the grenades were primed and the Bren magazines filled with tracer and ball. The boxes of grenades I had placed close to my trench so that they would be handy for me in the event of an attack. We had our usual stand-to that evening and I did a rather closer inspection than usual. I also advised Lieutenant Price to get another W/T set as the one he then had was not working. He had one sent up to him that evening. Funnily enough, I had had no message from H.Q. that this was 'the night', but perhaps this was due to Alan Redfern's influence, as I had already explained to him it made no difference to our organisation. We carried on doing our job in any case, so if the Jerry came tonight or in a few nights' time, it made no difference. Troops get tired of always being told to stand ready and I remember from my experience in the ranks that it leads to them rather not doing more than usual when such warnings are given. I felt convinced myself, however, that if Jerry was ever coming, he would make this the night.

CHAPTER 8

The Battle for Leros

I went to bed early. When I say early, it must have been almost 2000 hours. I was usually in bed before 2200 hours, in any case. I had no sooner got into my sleeping bag, than the lookout announced that seven or eight ships were approaching from the Turkish coast. I immediately got up again and with Price went out onto the lookout position. It was a glorious night with full moon and the moon, slightly to the east, had made a beam on the water stretching from us to the Turkish coast. We could see everything, and there, sure enough, were ships approaching at speed from the east. I immediately ordered a stand-to and signalled H.Q. The ships grew closer and there were aircraft around. Lieutenant Price had ordered his guns to stand-to and as these ships approached and we still had no reply from H.Q., asked if he was to fire a shot in their direction. I told him, no, certainly not, we had reported their approach and it was now up to the Navy to identify them. As they got closer, we could see that they were M.L.s, though still did not know if they were ours or not. The leading one was quite close, however, and was firing at the aircraft, so we presumed that they were ours. Before we got a reply, the leading M.L. had got into the bay and was obviously expected. We got a reply to say the Navy were expecting these ships.

The last ship was still being bombed and machine-gunned and was returning fire when we noticed it swing round in a great circle to the left. It immediately signalled S.O.S., all of which messages we passed on to H.Q. It then signalled by lamp asking for a tow as the rudder had been damaged. We attempted to signal by lamp to the ships below but they must have also seen the signal as two

> M.L.s put out to sea again and made for the stranded ship, which was still circling.
>
> Before the M.L.s reached the one, however, they had put their trouble right and were now proceeding in a straight line for the bay. There were two ships still some way off close to Turkey, but as we presumed the M.L. must also know about these, we left it at that and returned to bed.

The 'M.L.' seen to be in distress was, in fact, British Yard Minesweeper 72 on a supply run. The vessel had been targeted by Dornier Do 217s and struck by a remote-controlled glide bomb. The explosion brought down her mast and knocked out the port Oerlikon, damaged the steering and left the ship circling helplessly. Two men were killed, five were injured and one was reported missing. ML 299 and Motor Torpedo Boat 315 put out from Leros to assist. Travelling on the latter was Lieutenant Commander Ramseyer. He boarded the minesweeper, assumed control, and with the steering gear temporarily repaired, piloted the vessel into Alinda Bay.

> At about midnight, the lookout again woke me to say that there were two ships to the east and they were exchanging shots. I dressed and went out. It was quite obvious that an enemy ship was in the vicinity, although on one previous occasion, one of our own ships had been mistaken for enemy and shelled by one of the M.L.s. It was still some way out to sea, and, the moon having got over to the west, it was almost impossible to see anything. I reported this to H.Q. and returned to bed. I hardly slept, however, and got up at 0300 hours to go out and join the lookout. There was quite a Naval battle going on below us but still some miles out to sea. The Navy was obviously heading off approaching ships.

The reason for the night's activities would soon become apparent. It was Friday, 12 November, and the long-awaited German invasion was underway. Some 2,300–2,700 assault troops were to arrive between 12 and 16 November, considerably fewer than defending Allied forces, but also battle-tested and therefore more experienced.

In the early hours, two Wellington bombers of 38 Squadron had attacked the Kos flotilla, albeit without effect. Soon after, air reconnaissance – probably the same Wellingtons – reported fifteen 'barges' in two groups steering north-west from Pserimos, inside a minefield to the east of Kalymnos. The report seems to have been considered as relatively unimportant, and, in any case, the threat posed by sea mines precluded a pre-emptive strike by the Royal Navy. The Kos flotilla was soon joined by the force from Kalymnos. Both units then proceeded on course for Leros. Another bombing attack, this time by a high-flying aircraft, passed almost unnoticed.

The night's events were only just beginning. After landing dead and injured at Alinda, BYMS 72 was again underway, having been ordered to Portolago for repairs. In the dark, the minesweeper bypassed the port entrance and continued south, and away from Leros. Nearing Kalymnos, the minesweeper had the further misfortune to encounter the western landing force. Mistaking the enemy for friendly forces, those on the minesweeper were dismayed when they suddenly came under heavy fire. Three of the crew were killed and several wounded, the latter including the CO and first lieutenant. Both officers, together with fourteen ratings, were taken prisoner. Three men escaped after slipping overboard and swimming to Linaria Bay on the west coast of Kalymnos. The minesweeper, apparently with secret code books intact, was taken under tow to Kalymnos.

There was more action off Kalymnos when MTB 307, on passage from Kastellorizo to Leros, came under fire after challenging two German destroyers. The MTB took avoiding action, continued to Leros, and there joined MTBs 315, 266 and 263. All would later reach the safety of Turkish waters.

Shortly before 0500 hours, ML 456 sighted while on patrol the eastern invasion force 12 miles east of Leros. On approaching the vessels, the launch was engaged by an escorting *Räumboot* (minesweeper) and set on fire. The skipper hastily withdrew to Leros. Of the seventeen-man crew, one had been killed and six were wounded. Four of the more seriously injured were put ashore at Alinda, following which ML 456 departed for the Turkish coast. When barely 2 miles from Leros, she was mistakenly targeted by the island's shore batteries, struck by a shell and severely damaged. The battered little ship reached the sanctuary of Turkish waters soon before dawn.

Of three remaining motor launches that departed Leros in the early morning hours, MLs 299 and 461 arrived at Turkey without mishap. ML 358 is thought to have been caught between crossfire of the invasion fleet and shore batteries on Leros. The boat was lost, together with eleven of the crew, five of whom became prisoners of war.

> At dawn we could quite distinctly see about twenty ships to the north-east and everyone stood-to. The Italians manned their guns and had everything ready. Their stand-to cry had always impressed me and went something like this: "Posta de Comtatimento Maratanique", which presumably meant, "Take stations for a naval engagement" and sounded well with one of the shell cases rung at the same time and giving out a deep bell-like ring.

The Italian order was probably, '*ai posti di combattimento*' – a call to man battle positions.

> Everyone was in position but it was considered that the boats were still out of range. Lieutenant Price had taken up his position in my trench and I had taken up a position behind the No. [---] gun.
>
> The Navy then withdrew from the battle and we were able to see two destroyers, several landing craft and a Greek sail boat or two.

In all, the invasion flotilla comprised some twenty or so landing craft of various types, two small assault boats and nine escort vessels. There were two landing groups. The smaller of these approached Gurna Bay, but was turned back by shore defences. The remaining sixteen or so landing craft, escorted by four warships, including two destroyers, continued towards the northern shore and in full view of those at Battery Ciano.

> All the ships were making zigzag courses and gradually coming towards the cove which was below our gun depression.

> There was suddenly a tremendous bang and No. 2 gun had fired its first round at the destroyer, which was close in by now. This boat immediately turned about and went out to sea as fast as it could, putting down smoke as it went. The enemy's objectives were obvious: the cove below us already mentioned [Palma Bay] and the dead ground behind the hill to our north-east [Pasta di Sopra]. All guns were now firing and we could hear the 25-pounder shells as they whistled overhead. Our own Italian guns were doing splendid work and the shells went away with a tremendous rush. One could watch them for some way, they seemed to travel so slowly. It was all very exciting and we could only watch as everything was still well out of our range. I think the Italians had the first hit and sank a landing craft just as it was about to disappear out of sight behind the headland. This made the enemy hesitate and one or two of the landing craft then turned about. One of these craft had come in close to the island [Strongilo] which was opposite our bay. This was just the 25-pounder target as they had ranged on that very spot only a few days before. And sure enough, they had it. There was a tremendous explosion and in a few moments there was no sign of a craft where this one had been. I think this boat must have contained transport of some sort, as it was obviously making for a small road which comes in close to the shore a few hundred yards further up the beach. I do not know if anyone was saved from this boat. They may have reached the shore of the island, as they were close enough.

The destruction of *Pionierlandungsboot 'H'* resulted in heavy German casualties. Of two officers and fifty-one other ranks – most or all of 8. Kompanie/Luftwaffen-Jägerregiment 22 – just four ORs rejoined their battalion after the fighting was over. Thirty-two were taken prisoner and evacuated by the British. The remainder were killed or unaccounted for.

Another landing craft entered Palma Bay and disembarked two platoons of 5. Kompanie/Grenadierregiment 65, immediately below and within Bren gun range of those at Battery Ciano. The landing craft withdrew, leaving German infantry on a small pebble beach at the end of a narrow gorge in plain view of those above. The ground rose steeply on their left. On the right, the lower slopes of an ascending ridgeline seemed to offer at least some cover. In order to continue inland, however, it would then be necessary to expose oneself to fire from Clidi.

Feldwebel Gustav Wehrs would recall that the landing craft had come under heavy fire during the run-in, causing it to veer off course:

'We took cover behind the boat's bulwark and temporarily gave up our cover only when we fired our rifles, SMGs and machine guns; then the boat beached briefly and we jumped overboard onto land. The wireless operator was in front of me – I gave him a nudge as he was not moving: he had been hit, and to top it all, our second wireless operator also got his when he jumped. So, all contact to the battalion was cut off. Apart from these two, other comrades had fallen victim to the enemy defences. When I tried, as requested by the *Kompanie Führer*, Leutnant Drabant, to assess our numbers I could account for only 16. However, in the heat of the moment I had missed a few as each man had to look out for himself and find cover behind little rocky ledges. Our *Fährprahm* withdrew and we were left behind – a small group in a small rocky cleft of this inhospitable island.'

From Clidi, not 1,500 yards distant, the LRDG brought their Brens into action, opening fire on the retiring landing craft and troops alike. Olivey had a grandstand view of events:

> They returned machine-gun fire and we could now hear the bullets whining overhead. We had the advantage here, as it was well in range downhill, but only just in range uphill. Also, we could see the [muzzle] flash some time before the bullets arrived. They managed to put up quite an effective fire, however, and must have landed about four [machine?] guns and a few rifles. Some landing craft had also landed in the dead area and we could do nothing about this. The only thing was to engage targets we could see out at sea. The drill seemed to be for the landing craft to bring more men from the sailing boats, while the destroyer kept off possible M.L.s.

> There seemed to be very few aircraft about and what there were, were mostly engaged in air cover for the ships. Far off we could see more ships coming up from the direction of C. The Germans were able to disappear from sight having landed and were, no doubt, working their way up the river bed to the north-east. I had not sufficient men to allow for sending out a patrol to the far hill, though this is what I should have liked to do. I had considered early in the night sending a patrol onto the far hill to overlook the very spot at which they had landed, though, with Bren only, they will have been very little use. I could now see Germans moving up the hill opposite us and they installed a machine gun on the hilltop north-east from here. They were all to engage our troops in the forward trench and rather make Lieutenant Price's observation less simple.

With German troops now facing his own position from high ground 1,200 yards away, Olivey became less concerned about those who had come ashore at Palma Bay. In the event, the latter would become engaged in a battle with 18 Platoon D Company of the Buffs. Wehrs described the outcome:

'The British were positioned a short distance from us further uphill and gave us a hard time. Sometimes, you could even see them as they handled their guns. They had trouble depressing the gun barrels to aim at us. The shells went whizzing past closely above our heads. But they succeeded with their mortars and light weapons. A runner a few metres from me was hit. "Herr Feldwebel, I am dying," he said to me with blood gushing from his mouth after each word – a truly extraordinary situation. Eventually, Feldwebel Steinbach managed with another comrade to climb onto the ledge on the right side and once there had to defend himself with pistol and hand grenade against the Tommies, who – it would have been about 1500 hours in the afternoon – all of a sudden were among us. "Wehrs, now what?" Leutnant Drabant exclaimed in his characteristic Silesian accent. "I suppose this might be the end," I replied. Then Leutnant Drabant said to the British: "You are surrounded by 2,000 Germans." This was met with a ready response: "Yes, and behind them there are 10,000 English."'

When the Buffs returned to D Company location at Blefuti they brought with them at least forty-seven prisoners. For his actions that day, the platoon commander, Lieutenant Eric J. Ransley, would be awarded the Military Cross. It was a very different story for Olivey and his men, as German troops moved ever closer to Clidi.

> They were moving up all the time and now brought a mortar to fire on us, engaging the forward trench. One boat [sic: bomb?] landed very close. I could see their men every now and then over the hill, as in a long stream, walking in file. They were carrying mortar bombs up to the hill east of us [Point 278]. I was [sic: had?] several shots with a rifle and brought a machine gun to bear on their line, but they were able to move slightly farther over the hill and thus out of sight. As an infantry corporal, I should have had a range card of all these ranges we had fired on before. Now, I had to rely on my memory for the different ranges.
>
> At this stage, our own infantry arrived in jeeps on the hill west and I went back to talk to their O.C., a Major M. [sic: Major William T. P. Tilly]. I asked him to send one platoon forward to the right and one to the left. He could keep one on the hill to the rear in reserve. This was decided upon.

Fully appreciating the importance of holding Clidi, Brigadier Tilney had decided to reinforce the post with the Fortress Reserve, C Company of the King's Own. Contrary to Olivey's impression, few vehicles were available, and a good number of these troops arrived at the Italian barracks only after a long, tiring march. It was not long before the area was subjected to mortar and machine-gun fire and low-level aerial dive-bombing.

After conferring with Olivey, the company commander positioned 13 Platoon with two Vickers machine guns atop a ridge just behind the Italian barracks west of Battery Ciano. The location overlooked Palma Bay, with a view of enemy positions to the north. The two remaining platoons appear to have been tasked with a flanking attack in the direction of Point 278: 14 Platoon was directed left (presumably north of the feature), and 15 Platoon was sent right (traversing the southern face). Lacking local knowledge, the King's Own troops were expected to find their way over rocky, very rugged ground, while hoping to avoid German observation. Unsurprisingly, the plan went awry almost from the start.

> The platoon to the left hardly got forward at all before they were under fire and withdrew to the hill at the rear. The platoon on the right were far too far back and I asked if they could not go forward. This was ordered. Imagine my disappointment when about half an hour later, I saw them about 1,000 yards to the right and quite 800 feet below us. They would never be on the neck in time and would come under the direct fire of the enemy when they started to climb up again. I offered to send my sergeant down to show them the best way up, but Major Tilly thought they would find it themselves. What happened to this party eventually, I do not know, but I know they never got round to the right. The platoon on the left was now brought over to the right and got forward as far as the trenches. Some mortar fire rather upset them and I found the whole lot streaming back to the hill in the rear. I pleaded with their officer, but to no effect, I fear.

Olivey was justifiably concerned about the route taken by 15 Platoon. In 1945, the remains of the platoon commander, Lieutenant Desmond P. R. Ginn, were recovered from low ground half a mile south of Clidi, and far from his objective.

> In the meantime, Lieutenant Price had had his telephone line cut by a mortar bomb and the wires of his W/T set had been damaged. He had to withdraw and try and get his phone through again. This gave us no communication with the guns, just when we needed them, and I could not bring fire to bear on the mortar.
>
> I passed a signal to H.Q. asking Jake to get the infantry to go forward and received a reply to them advising them to do a recce

forward. This was sent addressed to two officers in the code names. No one knew who they were and no one wanted the job.

I had already advised Jake that the enemy were on the hill opposite. Lieutenant Price now asked for fifteen rounds of fire at a spot which he signalled. This we passed by my set and out to H.Q. Heaven alone knew when we would get it. As no one looked like doing the recce, I myself went forward to the front trench. I found the enemy on the neck of the hill below us and moving up from the coast. I knew they were on the hills opposite. I put all this in a report and signalled it as having come from me. I also signalled that landing craft were landing at the old castle and that our guns were engaging them.

At this time, only one, the No. 2 gun, was operating and 2nd Lieutenant Pizzigoni was doing grand work with this all round his front. He seemed to have been deserted by his crews, except for one man, and he and this one man were carrying shells and loading, aiming and firing, getting very hot over it. I laid on three men to carry shells for him. He was able to drive off two landing craft again approaching from the north.

The infantry were now all back on the hill behind and I sent a message to Jake imploring him to do something to get the infantry to stay on the hill with us.

Bennett and I went forward to the trench in front and there we could see the Germans starting up our hill.

From his brief description, it seems that Olivey and Andy Bennett took up temporary positions in a stone sangar situated slightly below and at the forward (northern) edge of the gun battery. German infantry would have had to approach across gently sloping ground that offered no cover whatsoever.

The commander of their detachment was standing in the open shouting up to us, "Hi, Aussie". Bennett got his Bren trained on him and we saw him drop. I left Bennett with his M.G. and promised to send another man to support him. I sent Olepse [sic: Rifleman Louis J. N. Oelofse]. Not long afterwards, Bennett received a bullet in the flash eliminator of his gun. This sprayed him with bits of metal and blood was pouring from his face. I sent him back after the medical orderly had advised this course and had bandaged him up. My shelter at the rear had proved very valuable, as one bomb had dropped very close and the sandbags no doubt saved the occupants' lives. This was now being used as our advance Bren post. Sergeant Calder Potts was now with Ox in the trench on the right and was able to engage the enemy on the hill opposite. The enemy soon spotted his position and had a sniper trained on him. Sergeant Calder Potts received a spatter of rock in the face which necessitated his withdrawal for the time [being].

We now received a signal from the Brigadier saying that Pt. 320 would be held at all cost. This I passed over to Major Tilly as I knew it was my reply from Jake. This time we were able to get a platoon to occupy the forward trenches and so could at least engage the enemy below us, though the snipers on the opposite hill kept their heads down very effectively. Bombing was now very considerable and I noticed that No. 4 gun had been knocked out. I received a message from the Brigadier that their guns would not be blown until ordered by him. This was afterwards cancelled as communications were so bad.

Signalman Bremner [James Bemner] was doing splendid work at the fort and I was able to slip in and have a word with him every now and then. The gunfire always sounded much worse in the fort and he complained of a headache. It was a beastly position, being impossible to see any action and getting the full benefits of it. He was doing splendidly and I told him so. I received a message from Jake saying that my information was most useful and had proved most timely and accurate. It put great heart into me, but Jake was always very understanding in those ways. I sent back a message that the infantry were now up with us and added that I thought the enemy were about company strength, adding something cheery: "a nice place you've got there", a little joke Jake and I always had. I scored fifteen points by saying it first.

2nd Lieutenant Pizzigoni was fighting like a demon. He had now carried the Scotti out into the part where he could engage the enemy in front and he was busy firing this gun completely in the open and with great courage. An enemy bullet jammed this gun shortly afterwards, however, and he returned to his No. 2 gun again and engaged the enemy on the far hill with this, but without much effect.

It was about noon or shortly after. There was a bit of a lull in the battle and I first noticed a distinct hum in the west on the skyline. I could see a low dark cloud very close to the sea and stretching about a mile wide. I looked again. The cloud was moving rapidly closer. There was a great stillness in the air. The cloud came closer and closer, and as it approached, it seemed to close in in the centre and got higher in the centre. The thought at once rushed through my brain – parachute troops.

It was a truly wonderful sight, this dark cloud of aircraft moving in perfect formation, looking at first as though a giant had stretched out both hands with fingers pointing and one and all in line, and then moving one hand above the other to form a solid mass of pointing fingers.

Everything was silent, every man on his gun, every gun pointing in their direction. I shouted, "Paratroops!" and ordered every gun to fire just below the aircraft. They approached almost on a level with us, or slightly below, and each plane seemed to be just missing the one in front or to the side of it. It was a truly wonderful sight.

And then as the first man jumped, everything on the island seemed to open up at once. Bullets flew overhead from our troops below. Everyone seemed to be firing. I'm not sure the officers didn't fire their revolvers. I had a Bren which got rid of three mags in almost no time. Three planes had crash-landed into the hill below us and two into the sea. It was impossible to estimate the number of planes, but, roughly, I should say fifty in all. Each troop carrier, about thirty in number, dropped about ten men, and after our recent [parachute] course, it was instructional to watch how fast Jerry came out of the planes. Many of the enemy dropped in the sea. Many never got up again, but those that did very quickly disappeared from sight. It was a perfect day for the manoeuvre and it was excellently carried out. A few planes had to come back to

> drop odd men who obviously hadn't made it, and, certainly, how they had avoided being struck by the plane behind was a wonder I shall never forget. One must give the Germans top marks for that performance, which was a wonder I never expect to see again from such a perfect position.

This, the first of two drops, was conducted by paratroopers of the Luftwaffe's I. Bataillon/Fallschirmjägerregiment 2. Of six Luftwaffe aircraft lost in the Aegean area on 12 November, only one Ju 52 transport is known to have crashed on Leros – below Clidi, on the northern shore of Alinda Bay. There was one survivor.

> They had landed just where we expected them. They formed up on the road in the centre of the island and I saw their H.Q. sign being fixed outside one small house. I signalled this position to H.Q. but why I did not open up with No. 2 gun on this house, I cannot for the life of me imagine. I rather think my attention was taken up in advising H.Q. when I could have done better myself in engaging the target. Every parachute troop seemed to report there before moving to the deep trenches south of this house – a perfect position. There seemed to be a lull in our own section, except that no one could look over the top without receiving a bullet from a sniper. It was about this time that Rifleman Oelofse was shot in the head and killed outright.
>
> As the afternoon wore on, I heard sheep grazing on our hillside, the tinkle of their bells sounding most homely in the battle.
>
> I immediately thought of Levitha and my previous experience, but dismissed the matter from my head.
>
> At this stage, Whitehead appeared with batteries for our set for which I had signalled. I gave him a complete map of the position in our area for Jake, marking the enemy position in red pencil, their lines of communication and landing spots in red, our own troops' position and where the infantry withdrew to in blue. I marked with pencil crosses where I should like artillery fire, and, with arrows, the likely advance of the enemy. I explained it all to Lance Corporal Whitehead at the same time. He set off back with

his jeep and was, I believe, the last car to get through before the enemy cut the road.

Signalman Clifford H. Whitehead did not survive the battle. He was killed during a bombing attack by Ju 87 Stukas three days later, on 15 November, and buried on the terraced slopes just below LRDG headquarters on Meraviglia.

H.Q. had now closed down and I could get no reply to my signals. I had to leave Bremner on the set for a while in the hope that he would get through. I afterwards gave him a rest and put W. [Acting Corporal L. P. Winter] on the set, but we never heard H.Q. again.

I went out into my position on the side of the fort and there saw the forward troops in their trench. I shouted to Lieutenant B. [I. L. Brown], whom I knew, to let me know if any enemy approached his position and I would support him with plenty of grenades. I went forward and brought an extra ton of grenades from my own trench. There were three or four infantrymen in the trench. I showed them the other boxes all ready for use.

Shortly before this, Lieutenant Pizzigoni had gone forward to the Z cave with a machine gun, having asked where the Germans were. It was almost impossible to see them as they were in khaki. I never saw 2nd Lieutenant Pizzigoni again. He had fought like a very gallant Italian soldier, and Italy could be proud of him. His commander had, I fear, withdrawn from battle, and, with another Italian officer, was sitting in the fort resigned to his fate. He was, I think, a bit old for war.

Daniele Pieri was 50 years of age. He would later be awarded Italy's Silver Medal for Military Valour (see Appendix iv). He and his second-in-command, together with other Italian officers taken prisoner on Leros, are believed to have been shot in compliance with Hitler's directive of 11 September 1943.

Towards evening, the sheep had grazed very close and there seemed to be no sign of the enemy in our area. They were, however, in evidence on the opposite hill and snipers continued to keep our heads down. I again reminded Brown that whatever happened to give us a shout and we would support him. I tried to keep on talking to these forward troops to keep in touch from my position. Although I could see them, I could not see the hill below them. I took a walk down to our trench going to the rear. The trench had been almost completely filled in and blown flat. There were no troops down in this area, but it could be covered from the rear hill where a platoon of the infantry were. It was impossible to get forward to No. 3 gun, as this was covered from the opposite hill. I went back to my position. I again shouted to Brown, who replied that he could not move as he was pinned down by fire. I told him to keep a lookout and I would support him until dark. I called him again about fifteen minutes later but he and his section had completely disappeared. Ox and the men with him had heard nothing. What had happened to him?

I then noticed that the Germans were working round to our left. Why did not the forward trench engage them? I found they had. Either all had been killed or were not there.

I went back for Major Tilly and advised that a platoon should put in a counter-attack to the left. This was decided on, and the infantry formed up. We gave covering fire as best we could from the right flank. The infantry could not get forward, however, as every time they moved, grenades and mortar fire met them. Major Tilly said he would take them forward himself. It was now about dusk and the enemy were on No. 3 gun position and below No. 1. We could hear the orders of the forward officer instructing the mortar how and when to fire. The bombs would drop most accurately at the feet of our infantry. The infantry made a charge but it was impossible to get to the Jerry's position over such rough ground. Major Tilly was wounded in the neck and went out of action. The infantry withdrew to their hill behind.

With the first German troops having reached Battery Ciano, the fighting became ever more desperate, as Rhodesians and Germans confronted each other at close-quarters.

> It now became a fight between L.R.D.G. and the Jerry. I had a Bren gun with which I could sweep our left flank and I was able to cause great havoc in a party of the enemy who had moved across to No. 4 gun. I took very careful aim and knocked out their leader as he crossed the wall. This made the enemy withdraw from this flank. They had also occupied my own trench behind No. 1 gun, and, using grenades, I was able to drive them out of this. They took up a position on the far and almost sheer slope of No. 1 gun emplacement, and from here they would make sallies forward, pelting us with grenades. They had, unfortunately, found my three boxes of grenades and we were getting a number of our own grenades thrown at us.
>
> It was impossible to dislodge them from their position, as no grenade would stick on the side of the emplacement, although we could hear from their warning shouts that there were men behind them and below who got the benefits. I was using my Bren like a Tommy gun now and a German soldier behind No. 1 gun was firing back at me. It was almost dark and neither of us could see our sights. We would both bob up to get a better view, fire a burst at each other, and down again. His shots were going a bit too high, although one struck the stones in front of me, giving me a gash on the cheek and mouth. We were fast running out of grenades and our position was most insecure, as any troops coming round to the right could now very easily get to us.

Olivey's actions would make a lasting impression on those who witnessed them. Jack Rupping recounted that when Olivey positioned himself atop the battery command post with his Bren, 'One of his men realised his danger and pulled him down.' Years later, Don Coventry recollected the same, or a very similar, incident: 'Capt[ain] Olivey climbed onto the top of the pill box to survey the area and had the binoculars shot out of his hands. Fortunately his only injury was to his face from splinters of the smashed binoculars.'

The situation was by this time extremely precarious.

> Bremner asked for permission to leave his set and the chaps pulled him out through the window. He had destroyed the set with his

rifle. He was only just out in time, as a Jerry must have worked his way up to the fort and fired in at the window. Bullets came out through the other window and completely destroyed the W/T set. I dropped a grenade over the other side and the Jerry ran and fell as he ran.

Things were getting very pressing and we could not hope to hold on, short of grenades as we were. We were now using Italian grenades – the little red tomato things which are almost useless except for making a loud report. I now gave orders to withdraw to No. 2 gun and we commenced to get back. Van H. [sic: Rifleman Johannes D. van Rensburg] had gone back to this gun and now reported that the fuse and charge were all ready for blowing the gun. We lined up on the steep side of the rear of No. 2 gun and waited for the enemy to appear, when we would give them our last grenades. I told everyone to keep well behind the gun emplacement as they were then safe from grenades. Van Rensburg was sitting on the gun. A grenade came over and exploded on the top of the emplacement and Sergeant Calder Potts, who had not got behind the emplacement, got the full benefits of the explosion in his stomach. I ordered two chaps to help him back and we gave the Jerries our last grenades. At the same time, van Rensburg pulled the switch.

This gave us thirty seconds to get away. We made [our way] back towards the hill to the west. The thirty seconds seemed like an hour and I almost thought that the charge had failed. But, suddenly, with a tremendous explosion which I knew would signal the fall of the hill to Headquarters, the gun blew up.

I collected my men and we went down to B. Squadron Headquarters in the wadi, having left Sergeant Calder Potts at the first aid post, and the infantry to hold their hill.

The battery had finally been taken by troops of II. Bataillon/Luftwaffen-Jägerregiment 22. German casualties included one officer, a senior non-commissioned officer and another soldier killed. That night, troops from 7. Kompanie secured the northern face; the engineer platoon of II. Bataillon/Grenadierregiment 65 took up positions on the southern slope. German forces now held the high ground from Point 234 at the northern end of the Vedetta feature, south-west through Points 228 and 320, and positions extending south-east from Clidi to about 550 yards west of Sante Madonne on the northern shore of Alinda Bay. With their paratroopers in control of most of the key points south of Clidi, the Germans had effectively divided the island in two.

CHAPTER 9

Counter-attack

It was a great disappointment to us losing Pt. 320 but everyone had done their best. It was, in any case, of very little value to the enemy now that only one gun, and that gun unable to fire on the Headquarters position, was left. We had a cold tin of Irish stew and some water, and, as the first meal that day, it tasted well. We then settled down for the night, having placed our guards out of men who had been out of battle all day.

On these occasions, I usually find myself getting up and listening half the night, so that I seldom get a good sound sleep and this night was no exception. I was continuously getting up, although there was nothing to get up for. I had ordered that we should all be called at 0400 hours so the night was short enough in any case. We then issued every man with a day's rations and his water bottle of water. I dispersed them around the hill and told them that they must keep a lookout down the valley, and should any enemy attack us, we would try to stop their advance up the hill. Surprise would be everything in this case, so that [meant] everyone must keep properly hidden. The day was uneventful for us. No enemy came. I did a short recce round the hill to within sight of the fort but there was no sign of enemy this side of the fort. Towards evening, I thought I saw a number of Germans approaching up the valley but these turned out to be Italians who were, no doubt, hiding in the trees.

Leros is frequently buffeted by fierce winds that can quickly increase to gale force. At such times, the exposed slopes offer little or no shelter from the elements. The noise can be such that it overrides any other sound. So it was on Saturday, 13 November. Olivey considered this fortuitous, however, as he believed that no German reinforcements would attempt to come ashore in such weather, and that it was quite impossible for another parachute drop. He was mistaken. At daybreak, an opposed landing was made by II. Bataillon/Grenadierregiment 16 near Pasta di Sopra. They were joined by part of III. Bataillon/Grenadierregiment 440, the troops landing north of Grifo Bay, before being directed south to link up with paratroopers at Rachi, in central Leros. One company also came ashore below Appetici, joining 1. Kompanie/Küstenjäger-Abteilung 'Brandenburg', who had arrived the day before. At 0645 hours, paratroopers of 15./4.Rgt. 'Brandenburg' and about forty of I./Fallschirmjäger-Rgt.2 were dropped west of Rachi. They suffered heavy losses. One stick was dropped at such a low altitude that none of the parachutes deployed in time. Ground fire accounted for at least two Ju 52s. Central Leros remained an area of intense fighting as defending British troops attempted to maintain a hold on hilltops and ridgelines extending south from Clidi to Rachi and east to Meraviglia and Appetici. For Olivey and his patrol, however, the day was largely uneventful.

> That evening, we collected together again on the hillside and organised ourselves into groups of three who were to move up and watch the road above us. One could hear the enemy moving up the hill – first a few mortar bombs, then some light automatic fire spraying the bush, then more mortar fire, and so on up the hill. It sounded as though they were moving up the hill to the fort and we hoped that we might be able to pick off a few as they passed along the road. We watched for some hours but [no] more passed. Then one of the men spotted movement up close to the fort, so I concluded that they had got past us unobserved. We gave them a few bursts of Bren and went back to bed. All night long, the movement went on. It sounded close, but must have been far away.
>
> I reported the movement to the C.O. in charge of this area first thing in the morning [14 November]. He would not believe it possible and said that his men were moving up all night and that

> an attack on the fort was planned to take place at 0600 hours. I asked for orders, as I could now not get in touch with my unit.

Earlier, Lieutenant Colonel Douglas P. Iggulden, commanding 4 Buffs, had been instructed by Brigadier Tilney to retake Clidi during the night of 13/14 November, following which he was to swing right and take the northern slopes of Rachi. Iggulden had already made up his own mind to restore the situation at Clidi, intending to commence the attack at dawn on the 14th. B Company of the Buffs were entrusted with the task. Olivey was told to report to the company commander, Major Ernest A. Hole.

> I returned to my chaps, divided them into two squads under the two Lance Corporals, took two chaps with me and left three at the camp. Funnily enough, those at the camp disliked their jobs most.
>
> The attack started on time and 3" mortar fire and gunfire from the 25-pounders opened up for five minutes. The infantry then went in and drove the Germans out of the fort, taking many prisoners. I then found Major L. [sic: Major Hole] and asked him for a job. He at once asked me if I could free the hillside in part, as Germans in the caves were holding up his advance and inflicting casualties whenever his men tried to get down.

Olivey ordered that as many grenades as possible be brought forward. He then issued instructions to Coventry, Rupping and van Rensburg, warning them to expect sniping from a nearby height and that Germans in the caves immediately east of Battery Ciano were firing at anyone who came into view.

> I proposed sending them down to the L cave on the right. They would then move round to the Z cave in the centre and engage the men while I slipped in with grenades. It didn't quite work out like that, as a Jerry with a sub-machine gun engaged me, while another engaged them. Still, I was able to see where he was and reach him with grenades. I prepared four and had them, ready, and next time Jerry came out, I dropped a grenade at his feet. It exploded after

the correct time. I dropped another with the same results. This brought cries of "*Kamerad*". I dropped another. They now set up a shout. I dropped another, this time with the pin in so it would not explode, gave them time to all be shouting again and dropped myself in front of them. They all put their hands up and looked surprised as I picked up the grenade. We had captured fifteen Germans in this cave and we trooped them all up to the top. Some of them were badly wounded and all were very shaken. It was a good bit of work and we felt pleased with ourselves. We made the prisoners take off their camouflage nets from their helmets so that their aircraft should recognise them. They produced small hard sort of dog biscuits, which they all carry as food. It was impossible to move some of the wounded without stretchers and transport, so we handed them over to the medical orderlies, and returned to Major Hole. The Germans had again suffered heavy casualties and we found the Colonel of this detachment mortally wounded in the fort. He had been hit in the chest, on the first day, so the prisoners told us.

The German 'Colonel' was probably Oberleutnant Böttcher, OC 7. Kompanie/Luftwaffen-Jägerregiment 22, who was wounded on 12 November. He is believed to have survived the battle.

Major Hole had decided to go round to the left of the hill, as he was now going to attack the hills opposite and so sweep round to L. I suggested that as our chaps knew the country, they might be useful as guides. This was agreed to and we attached ourselves, three to each platoon and myself with Major Hole. I fear our force was a bit too fast for them. The infantry are hardly capable of moving as fast as we had been trained to go. Also, perhaps, we got them a bit too dispersed. In any case, there were several holdups and Major Hole kept on saying that he was losing touch with his company, when it was only just out of sight round a hilltop. We brought them without mishap to within rifle fire of the enemy and here they had their first casualty. It seemed silly to me to attempt engaging the enemy when they were on top of the hill and could

> hardly be seen, and we were bound to have casualties if we stopped to fire. I pushed on and kept well away from their bunched ranks.
>
> We arrived at the top of the hill and the enemy had withdrawn to the far hill. It was now really an infantry job, and as we seemed to be messing them up in their job, I withdrew my chaps and let the infantry go on, saying we would meet them round to the right.
>
> Major Hole had hardly left me when he was shot dead. His second-in-command then commenced to lead the troops back down the hill. I rushed after him and implored him not to lose the advantage he had gained, but I could see that we were mixing ourselves up in a job we did not understand so, collecting my chaps, I ordered them all back to the fort. I seemed to suddenly fear that the enemy would counter-attack and re-take the fort. I started off across the valley. As I was in the middle of it, aircraft came over and with the special object of this valley. They had obviously been warned by W/T from their ground forces, and I think thanks to us, there were no infantry in the valley at the time – our advance had been too rapid.

Penned overleaf is one of several 'afterthoughts', together with instructions as to where they should be inserted in the original 'letter'.

> It had been impossible to call for aircraft by the rocket method, as we had captured their haversack of rockets and two pistols for firing these.

The narrative then continues.

> I saw the bombs coming and dropped in a hole. I was half buried with earth, but whole, and before the next wave arrived, I was running up the opposite hill back to the fort. I arrived back at the fort at about noon and found Lieutenant Price under a rock where we sat and smoked a cigarette and ate some chocolate.

Following the death of Major Hole, Lieutenant W. H. (Bill) Taylor took over command. Later, as a prisoner of war, he wrote:

'In the attack on Clidi my platoon was left forward platoon, 2/Lt. [Thomas L.] Morgan with 12 Platoon was on the right, while Lt. Dusty Millar with 11 Platoon gave us supporting fire from behind and slightly to our right.

'During the attack 2/Lt. Morgan was fatally wounded and died within half an hour. One of my men was killed and several wounded including two of my section commanders.

'On Pt. 292 our company commander, Maj. Ernest Hole was killed and I was in command of the company when we withdrew to Clidi where Capt. [Anthony D.] Tony Wood took over command of the company.'

There is no Point 292 in the Clidi area. But from the location of field burials located in 1945 and battlefield debris found in recent years, it is possible to determine that the Buffs got as far forward as Point 228, north-east of Clidi and just short of the Vedetta feature. In addition to the casualties among 4 Buffs, Signalman Harold A 'Toddy' Todman of the LRDG was also mortally wounded.

During the day, X2 Patrol was reinforced by New Zealanders of T2 Patrol who arrived with Second Lieutenant Cross. The officer later returned to the Gurna Bay area, leaving five men with Olivey.

> A New Zealand machine-gunner of our unit was fixing up some Vickers and had these well-positioned for defending the fort, but when the enemy worked back on the hill opposite, these positions were impossible and one gun was damaged. I contented myself in now defending the fort and visited my old office again. Everything had been turned upside down. My photos and frames had gone. Everything of any value had been taken. The place was full of dust, grenades and dead. Some Jerry had spilt a tin of fish over my bed and it stank of rotten oil. I put on two men to clear the dead out and clean the place up a bit.
>
> I could see our infantry wasn't moving round on the road to the north, so they had failed to dislodge the enemy. They were moving with a lot of Italians and a number of Germans, so they had taken a few prisoners.

> That evening a company of infantry came up to occupy the fort area. I had my men stay out on the hill behind, with a pre-arranged signal should I need them to come in with grenades.

It had originally been intended for B Company of the Buffs to push on to the north shore of Alinda and there link up with the battalion's C Company, which was expected to arrive by way of Quirico, a feature south of Clidi. This was not to be. When forced to abandon a position, it was standing operating procedure for the Germans to immediately counter-attack. As soon as Clidi had changed hands, therefore, II./Lw.-Jg.Rgt.22 was ordered to retake the height. The first assault was unsuccessful. A second attempt, this time with reinforcements from II./Gren.Rgt.65, also failed. So, the troops pivoted north and instead cleared Point 228 of any remaining Buffs.

> Just before the moon rose, a platoon of infantry was ordered to go out in front and hold a piece of the coast, so that no forces of the enemy would communicate between the east and central sectors. They were a bit slow in starting and the moon had risen before they left. This was a pity as the enemy would certainly see them coming. I slept that night on top of the fort. There was no disturbance except that supply dropping on our fort and bombing on the enemy's fort was taking place. A destroyer came in early in the evening, sank a landing craft which was near the north-east shore of the bay, shelled the centre of the island and went out again. It then moved round to the north-east, where the enemy had landed, seemed to remain there for some little while and then put out to sea. I still presume it was a British destroyer, though much discussion took place on this point.

Late that afternoon, HM Ships *Penn*, *Aldenham* and *Blencathra* had arrived off Leros with instructions to bombard enemy shipping at Alinda. The destroyers engaged three caiques, before turning their guns on German defensive positions. The bombardment continued for about fifteen minutes, during which both enemy and friendly forces had to take cover. The hospital at Villa Belleni was hit, resulting in the deaths of several patients. There were also casualties among C Company of the Buffs. The disruption was such that the company commander considered it impractical to press on and instead pulled back to reform south-east of Quirico.

After dark, a patrol of HQ Company of the Buffs moved into position on Point 111, between Quirico and Clidi, thus strengthening the British line, which extended from Clidi, south-west through Quirico to Germano on the northern shore of Gurna Bay. The ground from Meraviglia west to 'Searchlight Hill' (at the southern end of Rachi) was in Allied hands, and, so far, the Germans were contained on Appetici. To avoid being cut off, German troops were pulled back from the north-west slopes of Meraviglia and the line extending to Santa Marina (on the southern shore of Alinda Bay), to a line from Rachi, north to the coast near Patriarcato. A company was also deployed just north of San Quaranta in the area of Villa Belleni.

CHAPTER 10

Holding the Fort

It was now Monday, 15 November.

> I woke early and commenced to build myself a hideout on top of the fort. I collected all the sandbags I could and built up a wall 2 feet thick and 2 feet high, with slits through which I could watch the whole front of the fort. I covered this over with some wooden slats, and stones on top of that, as camouflage against air [attack]. I was then able to watch the whole front with bullet proof protection from the front and hidden from the air. It was an excellent spot and I should have had it before. I had covered the front of the bags with stones, so that the enemy would never spot it.
>
> Just before [first] light, I borrowed a Tommy gun and went down to the cover in front. I was frightened someone might have come into there during the night. I first visited the L cave and rather curiously went inside and struck a match. There was no one there. I thought I was rather foolish as they would obviously see me first. Why hadn't I brought someone with me? Should I go back? I must say, I was rather frightened.

Olivey deliberated his chances, deciding he would risk entering the Z cave. This was situated only a few yards away.

> When I reached the next cave, something told me to beware. Then a husky German voice said, "*Herr Doktor! Herr Doktor!*" as though badly wounded. Almost at once came back, "*Es ist kein Doktor hier*" ["There is no doctor here"], but before he had finished, my Tommy gun fired six or seven rounds into the cave. Two Italians,

whom I recognised, came out telling me not to shoot. I told them to bring the Germans out.

Two very shaken German soldiers emerged, and implored Olivey not to shoot.

I told the Italians to bring out the rest but they claimed there were no more there. What a fool I was not to have brought another man – I could not possibly go in the cave now.

So I proceeded with these two up the hill and the Italians brought up the rear. I questioned the German prisoners, who put up their hands every time they saw a British soldier! They told me that there were only four men on the other side, and they had no water. It was days after when it dawned on me that they were still referring to the cave. I gave them water and sent them off to Battalion Headquarters with a man who spoke German, but I understand the infantry were not interested. The figure of four was repeated.

With the infantry platoon was John W. C. E. and he had taken a walk down to the forward [trench?] of No. 3 gun during the early morning. He had found a German officer almost dead and unconscious and another very depressed with a bad wound in his foot. He had come back for water, but was unable to find a stretcher to get them out. Sniping started and he could not get to these two officers again that day.

John W. C. E., who Olivey also refers to in an after-action report as Lieutenant John Warner GC, was evidently quite a character. Unfortunately, there are no other clues as to his identity.

We had a day of being continuously bombed and reporting on the happenings of other troops in the centre of the island, I was able to put in a fairly constant report to the colonel of the battalion down the hill. I had persuaded Lieutenant Price and Lieutenant John F. [John L. Freeman] to bring the telephone back up to the fort, as it was far more use up here. The material could be supplemented with Italian telephone wire. We were able to study the German methods very well. The ground to air communication was done by a coloured rocket for the day, fired directly over the enemy position. The Stukas, who would cruise around overhead, sometimes for an hour or so, would, if their petrol supply was giving out, ask for targets by firing one rocket as they left the German position. If the infantry wanted support before this time, of course, they got it, as the pilots were obviously on the lookout all the time. The Ju 88s were advised either beforehand or by W/T and usually had pre-arranged targets. This arrangement of Stuka support obviously upset our infantry attacks, as the bombing could be called up any time and very quickly, and though not as accurate as shelling, was most effective. We were able to watch their infantry or parachute troops against our own. The British would force the Jerry into some rough ground where they hoped to corner them, then either one Jerry would break through our lines and bring up support in the rear of the British lines, or the whole of the Jerry party would go to ground and remain concealed in the bush, so that when the Tommies advanced, they would often go right through them without seeing them and the Germans, thus released from their tight corner, would take up better positions in our rear. It was very disappointing to watch this time and again happening.

We watched several actions which were successful to the British, however, and in ordinary country there would have been no doubt about the outcome of the battle. This day it was the object of our troops to swap from north to south and except for their tactics of breaking back, it was going well. The Jerries still owned their Headquarters, however, and had machine-gun posts all round it.

Making use of the German signal pistols they had acquired, Olivey tried to trick Stuka pilots into bombing their own troops. But without knowing the correct firing sequence, his efforts were in vain.

I was never successful. I noticed that when the Germans were successful, a donkey was always much in evidence with its braying.

> On our own hill, the enemy had laid a machine gun on a fixed line to fire just outside our fort door. I therefore posted two men to warn everyone and make them either go round another way under cover, or to hurry across the gap. The bullets took about two seconds to arrive after they had run, so one was safe, and we had no casualties from this, though several were frightened. We fired back most of the day, but the enemy gave us very little target [opportunities]. We seemed to be the spare target for bombers as, whenever no other target presented itself, we got the benefit of bombs. That evening, John W. went forward to collect his wounded German officers. Imagine his surprise when he found the one with a wounded foot very cheerful and the unconscious one gone. They had no doubt been having a conference which John had interrupted and there was most likely nothing wrong with the other one! The company commander had been told to send out a patrol to find out why nothing had been heard of his patrol of the previous night. I asked George Jellicoe, who was now my O.C. as I was out of touch with Alan, if I might send out this patrol under an officer. He gave permission. Lance Corporal Coventry, Rupping and van Rensburg went with an S.A.S. officer. They searched the valley almost to the coast, but found no trace of the missing platoon. They were fired on by the enemy at one spot however.

While it is questionable if a patrol or platoon was unaccounted for from the night before, certainly, a search party was dispatched the following afternoon, when Lieutenant Denis Millar and 11 Platoon failed to return from a standing patrol towards Grifo Bay. Those detailed for the task were joined by a 4 Buffs officer, Lieutenant M. H. (Mick) Gurmin. ('Dusty' Millar showed up later as a prisoner of war.)

> Early next morning [16 November], I sent a party of three under Lance Corporal R. [Rupping?] down to the caves, but this time no one was to be found. I had reason to ring up the C.O. of the area early that morning and I could distinctly hear someone listening in on the line. From now on, we were constantly through

> by telephone to San Giorgio at the other end of the island. As the telephone line ran through the enemy lines, it looked rather 'fishy'. I posted men in the caves this day with instructions that they should keep a lookout for anyone coming up the hill. Nearly everyone got in the caves in good time. Bremner and Foley [Private Kenneth Foley, medic] were, however, late, with the result that Bremner was sniped as he was crossing the barbed wire and received a wound in his foot. Foley dived after him, looking as though he had himself been wounded, but this was not the case. They decided they could fix Bremner's foot up for him and would stay there for the day under cover. I had tried to lay on artillery fire so we might get them out, but I lost the line [just] as I wanted to switch the fire. The L.O. [liaison officer] of the area rang up to say that he had received a message from Brigade saying, "hold your fire, we are evacuating." He asked me to keep a lookout to see what was happening. I could see men running about on Headquarters hill [Meraviglia], but it was very misty and I could only see to the north. I told him I had seen a few men running down to the north. He said he thought it was unlikely that the Brigade would come this way and gave reason that he had previously arranged to go south-east or west. His own position was very precarious with a very depleted battalion and a few Italians. He said that the position was deteriorating rapidly, but that he was putting in a drive to hold the enemy to the north. We were able to watch and report on many battles in the centre section. I received news from George Jellicoe than Alan had been killed. Jake was said to be holding the centre hills; Alan Denniff, San Giorgio – and ourselves, 320. So L.R.D.G. were in forward positions.

The LRDG second-in-command, Major Alan Redfern, had been killed on the first day of the German invasion, his role passing to Captain Alan Denniff. San Giorgio was held by Italian gunners together with New Zealanders under Second Lieutenant R. F. (Frank) White.

> John W. had offered to find out if there were any Germans still on the opposite hill by walking out in front and seeing if they would

Lieutenant John Olivey in the uniform of his parent unit, The Sherwood Foresters.

Olivey at Shepheard's Hotel, Cairo, after the award of his first Military Cross.

Captain Olivey.

Newlyweds John and Micky Olivey at Victoria Falls, Rhodesia, in November 1942.

Left to right: Johannes van Rensburg (killed in 1944), Don Coventry and Tommy Bradfield (latter wounded at Levitha). Coventry's role during the defence of Clidi earned him the Distinguished Conduct Medal.

Greece, 1944. Left to right: Captain Bill Armstrong, Captain John Olivey, Alf Page, Bill Cooke, Sergeant Don Coventry, 'Artie' Botha, Ben Harding, Tommy Haddon, Reo Armand and Colonel John de Lisle 'Jock' Thompson. More than half of these men were recent recruits to the LRDG. Not long after this photo was taken, Rifleman Botha was shot dead and Captain Olivey was wounded.

shoot at him. I could not allow this mad plan! I was certain they were still there and I was proved to be right as two mortar bombs came over shortly before sunset.

It was a day of many excitements. At sea, I saw an M.L. attacked by three Stukas and sank in about sixty seconds, leaving no trace. As John and I were coming out of the fort, a bomb landed right at the door, driving a tremendous wind down the passage, which sent a stream of tin hats, caps, etc. whistling along. The whole place was plunged into darkness as black as night. Everyone thought the fort had collapsed, but gradually the dawn came again and we found that it was just dust which had caused the darkness. John said it beat London any day [...]

I had just offered to purchase his sniper rifle for a tot of whisky and we were about to go and drink it, so now was a good time. We sat down on a rock and had a mouthful each of whisky. I had had a bottle but the German colonel had been fed on it.

We had a good talk for about half an hour and John gave me a German automatic he had taken off the officer. I showed him how good a shot I was and knocked a carton in half at 25 yards, rather to my own surprise. The sniper rifle I kept, as I thought I might get my own back at the Jerries on the other hill if they appeared. Orders now came that we were to man the fort alone and the infantry were going to put a sweep through to the south. We therefore got everyone we could firing while the infantry quietly moved out.

Unfortunately, Bremner and Foley decided to move up at this time and a Stuka, spotting them and myself and other men on the fort, made a dive, machine-gunning. Foley was hit in the legs and Coventry had to go down to bring him up. I had seen the flash of the gun and dived behind cover with a New Zealander none too soon as a bullet struck the place we were standing. I had proved I could move faster than bullets however!

I asked George how long I had to hold the fort. He told me until our casualties were heavier than the enemy's, which seemed fair enough. He also said that G. was trying to organise demolition parties. REFUE had already collected odds and ends of guns and

> W/T sets. He also told me that three Z-barges were stationed at x [Parteni?], should anyone need to get off the island. I was very much afraid the Jerries now had the information.

G. may refer to Captain Ashley M. Greenwood, liaison officer on Leros between the LRDG and Jellicoe. It is not known who or what REFUE was, nor the location of the following reference to P.E.

> He reported Jake's death and ended up by saying that he and the Colonel were going through to Brigade who had sent for them. I told him I thought it very risky, as the road was now held strongly by the Germans. A rumour passed on by Lieutenant Price was to the effect that seven enemy barges were in P.E.

Lieutenant Colonel Jake R. Easonsmith, a much-respected commanding officer, was shot dead during a night patrol on 15/16 November, following which, Colonel Guy L. Prendergast, OC Raiding Forces Aegean, had reassumed command.

Until they were told otherwise, the LRDG would continue to hold their positions: Headquarters remained at Meraviglia (No. 6 W/T post, call sign TJS), Captain Olivey at Battery Ciano (OP No. 2 W/T post, call sign NIN), Captain Dudley Folland and his patrol at Battery Farinata (OP No. 1 W/T post, call sign MPD) and Frank White at Battery San Giorgio (OP No. 4 W/T post, call sign YFB). Unlike at Meraviglia and Observation Post No. 2 atop Clidi, OPs 1 and 4 were fortunate not to have become directly involved in any fighting during the five-day battle.

> George rang up again to say that they were trying to organise a party to get off the island and we were to hold on and draw the enemy.
>
> I left the organisation of the guard to Lieutenant Freeman and turned in early, as I expected to be up early. I was sleeping at the top of the fort and heard the telephone bell ring. Lieutenant Freeman said I was asleep and he would take a message. I fell asleep before the conversation had finished. I woke up early

with what appeared to be Beaufighters dropping anti-personnel bombs. It was very misty and these bombs exploding halfway to earth were most unpleasant. I thought them Beaufighters on account of the sound and the fact that they made off back over Turkey, perhaps to Cyprus. They may have been enemy, however. The night was otherwise quiet, though there appeared to be a lot of aircraft about.

I went round the fort, and only got in front for a moment, when a machine gun opened up at me, fortunately striking a foot below where I was standing. I had been seen in the moonlight. I carefully planned where I should put my men and inspected No. 3 gun. I found that this appeared to be in good working order. I had asked Lieutenant Price to organise blowing this gun, but he said it was certainly out of order! I called my corporals together and put each (three) in charge of a party, giving one the right, one the centre and one left, with various jobs to do before dawn.

One of the jobs which had to be done was to remove a dead German who had been lying out in front and was getting very decomposed. In removing him, the troops found a German officer's note case. This was a most superior case of old and very soft leather, such as I have not seen since the 1914–18 war. It contained inside a row of pencils of every imaginable colour, a writing pad in small squares, very thick, and a note book with a leather cover and a monogram. The cover of the notebook had some positions of setting the various Headquarter signs to mean different things. The knowledge of the German language would need to be extensive to understand the abbreviations used. There were a few notes in German, but what caught my eye was a letter in English.

This letter, addressed to whomsoever it may concern, asked that in the event of his death, this letter be sent to the address given. The thanks of Lieutenant [name missing] was offered. My troops had brought this to me, and I accepted the case not knowing what was inside.

The unfortunate German was in all likelihood Oberleutnant Erich Frenzel, OC 6. Kompanie/Luftwaffen-Jägerregiment 22, who was killed at Clidi on the first day of battle.

> As it was getting near time to get in position, I woke up Lieutenants Price and Freeman, who had heard us moving about for some time. Lieutenant Price said, "Oh, don't worry, the show is over", and proceeded to tell me to report to [4 Buffs] Headquarters below. I told him that I had my orders, that the fort would be held. He started to argue and explain that this order had come through last thing. I had to do some quick thinking. Remember that I knew the line was tapped – I had had proof of it very recently when Alan Denniff had rung up to ask what his orders were. I told him I could not tell him – I meant the line was being tapped, but I fear Alan didn't understand. In any case, it was up to George to tell him. I knew G. [Ashley Greenwood?] had left.

Olivey must be mistaken in stating that he had received such a call from Captain Denniff, who, as the LRDG second-in-command, is unlikely to have asked a subordinate for instructions. The conversation is more likely to have been with Frank White or Dudley Folland.

> I decided I would not change my plan until I could see what the enemy were doing and what the position on the island was. In any case, I was not going to report to H.Q. if the show was over, and also I would get rid of Lieutenants Price and Freeman. I told them to go. Lieutenant Price started arguing. I ordered him to go. He went on arguing. Time was getting short and he was driving me desperate. In the end, he decided to go. Lieutenant Freeman came up and said good-bye. We shook hands and saluted Lieutenant Price and I was glad to see the back of him. He had been a little trial to me all through the battle, never doing the things I required done and all the time following me around. There are times in battle when one likes to get away by himself and think things out.
>
> I immediately returned to my troops and told them their various positions, that they were to remain perfectly quiet, and, if possible,

> not be seen from the opposite hill, to give the impression that the fort was deserted. Should anyone approach they were to wait until they were close enough to be perfectly certain of shooting him and would then shoot to kill. They had to be prepared to stay all day, though I hoped to relieve them before noon. I had received no written orders as promised and I knew that George would have ordered that I personally come to the phone, but on the other hand, would Lieutenant Price listen to any orders? I knew also that the L.R.D.G. had its escape plan which had obviously been altered on account of the three Z-barges. I had told my corporals that these barges were available for brave soldiers and I knew that most of my men had their own plan of escape.

Only the SBS and the LRDG appear to have formulated contingency plans in the event of a German victory. The LRDG were provided with five escape RVs. Parteni was additional to these and had almost certainly been arranged between Major Jellicoe and Lieutenant Commander Ramseyer to facilitate an evacuation of the SBS.

> We were all in position by dawn and all was quiet. We remained like this for about an hour, I continually watching the opposite hill and the village and road below, but there was no sign of life. A shot rang out from behind and I saw an Italian soldier who had been coming up the road throw up his arms, let out a yell, and run down the road again screaming. Coventry was in the position of this shot. He might have let him get a bit closer if he meant to kill him, but it didn't matter, it had given him a fright. But would he tell the Jerries?
>
> Now a number of seaplanes started leaving [...] and boats could be seen approaching the islands. The Germans started singing "*Deutschland über Alles*" in the village, so I presumed the battle was over.

Until the very end, the battle might have been won or lost by either side. But on Tuesday afternoon, 16 November, German troops overran Meraviglia, taking prisoner Brigadier Tilney and his headquarters staff. To avoid further bloodshed, Tilney decided to surrender. When the news reached those still holding out at scattered locations, most went quietly into captivity. Not so Olivey and his men.

> I now went back to my corporals and told them to advise everybody that they could, [to] now move out slowly, one by one, down the valley. They should remove the bolts from their rifles and the locks [sic: breech blocks?] from Bren guns and throw them away down the valley. They should take their revolvers if they could and as much kit as they could manage. They should move into the stones below the hill and stay put for the day, then move into the R.V. first thing at night and then to Cairo where we would meet on Christmas Day in the Rhodesian Club. I gave Corporal Coventry a map of the islands and Turkey. I told Corporal Rupping that I would meet him at the R.V. of B. Squadron, might be tonight, might be some other time, but not to worry about me as I would stay behind. They all then slowly began to move out and went so quietly that I began to wonder if they had gone.

CHAPTER 11

Wolves in Sheep's Clothing

Jack Rupping, who had been with Olivey at Levitha and Clidi, recalled their parting: 'When asked if he was coming with us, he replied that he had a letter to write to the GOC [General Officer Commanding] first. Captain Olivey was later seen by some of the men passing by the wadi. We made for the RV after dark.' Olivey had more important business to attend to, however.

> I moved into the fort and proceeded to put on some clean clothes and collect a few things together. It may have been thirty minutes before I heard the sound of sheep bells. Now there was something about these sheep bells that I didn't understand and I was determined I'd find out. I fixed up my dressing mirror, which was on the wall, on to a lot of wire in such a way as to be used as a periscope. I then stationed myself near a window. The sheep came closer and closer up the hill. I waited to see what would transpire, prepared for anything. Suddenly, a sheep sprang onto the top of the rise and started looking around. I could see nothing about this sheep in any way extraordinary, so I ventured to put down my glass and look myself. As I looked up, a Jerry appeared over the top and I could swear he held in his hand a grenade ready to throw. I got down again, but by the time I had picked him up in my glass, he had appeared on top and was followed by three or four others. There were now quite a number of sheep on top. The Germans drove the sheep on a bit and then, obviously deciding the fort was deserted, began signalling to the men back on the hill who had now appeared and were walking about. They never spoke a word as far as I could make out. At least, I never heard one. They all

had coats made of the German camouflage, [their] groundsheet which is so difficult to see in broken country. They came up to the fort and looked in the window, but by this time I had got flat up against the wall on the side of the window and I knew they could not see me. I prayed that no grenade would be thrown in on spec. I then heard them moving round to the other side, so, copying the actions of the German officer, I quickly slipped my arm out of my battledress and lay down on the floor, hiding my rather red face. I feigned to be dead. If they saw me, or not, from that side, I know not. In any case, they were not interested and moved off down the hill, taking with them my equipment and revolver, which I had left outside ready for when I went. I gave them time to get well down the road. I then decided it was time to get out myself. The sheep seemed to have gone off down the slope again, whether driven or because there was nothing to eat on the top, I could not say.

I therefore picked up a Tropal coat, a Jerry groundsheet, my sniper's rifle and [---], my Jerry automatic in my pocket, my Jerry colonel's note case, and, so laden, I set off. I walked boldly down the road and turned off down the valley to the right, where the troops seemed to have gone. I saw the New Zealand chaps a little way down the hill, sitting in the bush. I advised them to get better cover and myself moved off round the hill following a ledge. Here I found a spot well under the rock with some bush wood and grass. I covered myself over, putting the sheep skin with the wool outside and the Jerry groundsheet on top, and, covered with bush wood and grass, settled down for the day. I must have slept until afternoon, as the sun was well over when I was woken by sheep. I froze, not even daring to look at my watch. The sheep grazed by and were followed by a German who moved very quietly behind them like a shepherd. He looked straight at my cover, but as he was on the ledge below me, I hoped he had not seen me. Sheep and shepherd passed. Some thirty minutes later, very small little pieces of rock kept on falling on me from above and I felt certain that someone was dropping these on me. I never moved, although I was stiff in every joint, and soon the little rocks ceased to fall. What was it? I may never know. Was it the sun's heat breaking off little pieces of rock, or had that Jerry felt suspicious, which he was frightened to test out, as from my position I could have dealt with him very effectively if he had been below, and from on top he could do very little unless he had grenades. I stayed there, thinking what I should do and what would be my future plans.

Olivey remained where he was until evening. He contemplated his upbringing in England during the First World War, recalling fearful childhood memories of the German 'bogie man'. He also considered the situation in which he now found himself.

What, therefore, were my feelings now, when all looked as though it was over and I, through no fault of my own, had been beaten by the Germans? This, I feel, is what made me do the mad thing I then did.

Add to all this the fact that, since the war began, the husband of my childhood's best girl had been killed by a bomb in England and she, poor girl, had had her happiness spoilt.

I would have one more smack at the Germans! I very carefully got out the German colonel's writing case and wrote a note in which I asked that, in the event, my love should be conveyed to my wife. I apologised for not being able to stay for a drink, put my cigarette case – a wedding present from you – in the writing case and next to the German colonel's letter and closed the case up. I had, of course, given the farm address, as the cigarette case would not be sent until after hostilities.

Between this time and when it was quite dark, about an hour and a half, I thought out what I was going to do.

I expected to find the fort without any guards, as I had heard a carload of Germans go off down the road singing and it was unlikely that they would expect an attack so soon after we had been beaten.

I would, therefore, walk up to the fort, collect as much explosives as I could and with as long a fuse as possible would first blow No. 3 gun, which I felt sure was still in good order. I would then blow the main magazine, chiefly to cause a diversion. These should be blown at five minutes to eight, the hour I knew that the Z-barges were to move out with the escapees. If still no one appeared, I would try and burn down all the local magazines at each gun position. But I realised at the first explosion that Jerries would come up to see what had happened, but I would easily get away, knowing the hill as I did.

It was now quite dark, so I had a good look round and could see no one. I then put all my possessions in one heap, covered with the Tropal coat and Jerry groundsheet, put my Jerry automatic in my pocket and climbed up to the road. I stood and I looked long at the fort. There was no one about. I boldly walked up the road and down to No. 3 gun. There was no one there, so all was well. I then proceeded to pinch the explosive and charge which I knew were kept near the gun. I found them in the magazine, which was unlocked. There was quite a quantity, but not very much fuse. I could not find the pull switch which I knew van Rensburg had had for lighting the fuse. I also found that I had no matches with me, but I hoped I would find some in the fort. I then went back to the main magazine, and with the explosive I had, set a charge on top of the shell cases and piled some more shell cases on top of the charge. The whole job had taken about an hour but the moon had still not risen, so it was very dark. I took off my battledress coat. I do not know if the inventors intended that it should be so or not, but when a battledress coat is turned inside out, it makes excellent camouflage as the pockets and the linings are all different colours and the rough joins make the outline most indistinct. Besides this, it hid my pips on my shoulder which certainly were bronze.

I now went up to the fort to find some matches. I knew that I had hidden a box in my hideout on top of the fort – I would get those. I walked boldly up, but first had a look in my sandbagged hole, as I knew I had left a Tropal coat there and there might possibly be a box of matches in there.

The Tropal coat was no longer there. So, Olivey made his way up to No. 2 gun. On reaching the gun platform, he was surprised to see what appeared to be a large dog. Olivey stared and the dog seemed to transform into a sheep.

> As I looked at it, the thing seemed to get up on its hind legs and stand up like a crouching man, and the next thing it was a man and challenging me in German, "Wer geht dahin?" [Who goes there?]. Without thinking what I was doing, I approached quickly to this German, pulling my automatic out of my pocket at the same time.

In German, Olivey began to shout and swear at the bewildered soldier, berating him for failing to recognise his own colonel. He then took careful aim with his pistol and fired.

> I went to the front of the fort and [---] it, there was another. This one I shot at two or three times without saying a word.

(Olivey's narrative is not at all clear about what actually occurred with the two Germans he encountered. He implies that the first man survived, but in his 1944 interview with Major Cecil Mercer he clearly states that he shot and killed both.) Having well and truly lost any element of surprise, Olivey had little option other than to make a hasty withdrawal, leaving the guns and magazine intact. (The charges he prepared may have led to a still-unexplained explosion in March 1944, which left a huge crater at the site of what had been the main magazine.) As he strode back down the road, Olivey considered the implications of his actions.

> I suddenly realised I had got out of a very difficult position through no skill on my part, but through some power within myself working totally without my aid. I also realised that I had more or less committed murder, or at least that is what I felt at the time. I walked off down the road and turned down to where I had been sleeping all day.
>
> I sat down to collect my thoughts. It was obviously useless to go back as I still had no matches and the Jerries would now be on the lookout. I had better call it a day and get back to the R.V. As I

was thinking all this, a star shell was suddenly fired from the fort, which almost landed on me, but I was quite certain I could not be seen. Several of these were fired, obviously as a signal.

I thought I would collect my kit and get going, but this proved more difficult than I had at first thought and I could not find the ledge I was on before, search as I would. I was still looking, when a car arrived at the top of the hill. I specially did not want to lose my cigarette case and kept on looking, but the next thing I knew was that someone was whistling to me. I thought it was one of the New Zealand chaps and whistled back. Then I realised it was a German and I quickly moved off down the hill. The German came after me.

Now I do not think I mentioned that when I left the fort in the morning, I changed my double soled and [---] boots for shoes. This was a mistake I was to regret several times afterwards. Now was the first time, because I could no longer move quietly over rocks and rough ground. Nevertheless, I moved quickly and soon had left him out of sight. A star shell was fired which lit up the whole valley and I thought I saw men moving below me, but this may have been shadow. I say, however, that I had an excellent spot. The moon had now risen, but I was in the shade under a rock. Not only that, but there was a rock sticking up below me, which gave protection from the front. There were also large bushes in the area, one of which was close and to the left and [another] not quite so close, but to the right.

I got down here and remained perfectly still. There was not a sound. So I got up, picked up a large stone and a smaller one and sent the large stone rolling down the hill. Immediately, a star shell was shot up. The stone had stopped rolling, however. I then sent the small stone farther down the hill. The same process was gone through. It sounded most realistic although, at first, I had intended to find out who was in front. It now sounded as though I had moved down the hill. I then got down and decided I would not move for an hour at least. The next thing I heard were sheep approaching with their bells ringing. Now, for the benefit of those who will say I went to sleep and dreamt it, let me say that I put my head down to rest and found that the rock just on the right for my head was rather like resting one's head on the sharp end of a pencil, and even though I put my beret under my head, it was still most uncomfortable. Besides that, I was fully aware of my danger.

Out at sea was a red light showing from some ship off the Turkish coast. I realised that the Germans had put this out there so that any large ship crossing between the island and the coast would break the beam and so be seen.

I wondered if our Z-barges would realise this and at once appreciated that the Navy had most likely used the idea first.

As I was looking out to sea, I heard a great cheer go up from a caique which had drawn in near a destroyer out at sea. I had watched this caique put out from the bay at which the enemy had landed. I now wondered if I had got the wrong position for our Z-barges. I envied the British cheers, which must have been partly relief at finding the Navy. I thought it rather unwise, however.

The sheep came closer and closer, grazing, I supposed, as they came, and I was quite prepared for the shepherd to be a German soldier, as indeed he was, because it was he who fired the star shells. I could not see the sheep, however, although they were all around me at one stage. I was thinking more about not being seen than anything [else] to start with, but later I began to think what a clever scheme it was on Jerry's part to lull the enemy with sheep and move up behind them. This explained in a flash how John Kay had been taken at Levitha and how Brown and his party had disappeared without a word at 320 more recently, and how I, that very morning, might have easily been captured.

Olivey, exhausted after five days of battle, was by this time finding it increasingly difficult to think clearly.

Now I listened more carefully and I noticed a funny thing about these sheep and that was, although there seemed to be a large number of bells for a small number of sheep, yet they never all seemed to ring at the same time, and as I listened, something more struck me – that they always seemed to move and thus ring their bells in the same order.

Just then the shepherd wished to move on his flock and hit the stone with his stick, just tapping it. All the sheep stopped grazing and every bell was still, and after a pause of a few moments the bells would start ringing again.

A lamb bleated down the hill and the mother sheep ran off down to the lamb, as sheep do. As a farmer I took in all these finer points. Strange I had not noticed it was lambing time in Leros and very strange that a ewe should leave its lamb at night, even when being herded like this. I must have moved my head slightly, perhaps trying to look, and suddenly a [---] or some bird or other went off through the night with a swishing of wings, as birds do when flying fast. There seemed to be a mule on the opposite bank, and every now and then this mule would move, and every time it moved, it sent a number of rocks sliding down the hill. And then my thoughts turned to wondering if the Germans had, in some way, trained their animals as circus animals are trained and if they had a troop of performing sheep which could look for men, and I became convinced that this is what they had done. Is it possible that sheep could be trained to this pitch and what would be the use of them anyway? One could not be captured by a lot of sheep. The thing was ridiculous.

I heard the horse or mule whinny. Now, that is strange, because I've never heard a mule whinny.

I heard more sheep approaching from above and the sheep below move slowly further on. These sheep did exactly the same thing and I listened more carefully. They seemed to be in a sort of V-formation with the shepherd at the [side?] and behind. Now, I noticed that the sheep to the front-right rang the bell first, just a little tinkle, then the sheep to the left-rear would tinkle, then the left-front and then the right-rear, then the second right-front and the second right-rear, the centre-right and the centre-left and then it would all start again in the same order, with every now and then the shepherd calling for silence by tapping a stone, and a lamb bleating, calling its mother, and on the lamb bleating, the shepherd would run back a few paces and fire a star shell. I listened most carefully. How were they able to train these [---] sheep to do all

> this? And still I could see nothing, and if I moved, the bird with the rush of wings would fly past me.

Sounds carry far at night, heightening the otherworldly atmosphere of a barren, windswept landscape such as that around Clidi. Then, the surrounding hills and valleys can seem unwelcoming, almost threatening. While Leros is predominantly limestone, there is an abundance of low-lying vegetation. This provides a home to nesting birds, which are easily startled, resulting in their noisy, sudden appearance almost from beneath one's feet.

Although goats and sheep tend not to roam at night, Olivey was sure they were all around. Ordinarily, such animals tend to move en masse and can be heard approaching by the distinctive clanging of their neck bells. On being disturbed, or on noticing something unusual, these intelligent and inquisitive creatures will typically stop and stare, remaining perfectly still without making a sound, before considering it is safe to continue. For Olivey, alone and disorientated, the situation had become increasingly surreal.

> In all, three lots of these sheep sections passed me, all exactly the same, and why did the bird always fly right over my head? I could not make it out at all and it was driving me mad. This sound of sheep bells, these shepherds, these mules, or at least it seemed to be the same mule. Perhaps it was the same bird, though I never heard it fly back. All sorts of things passed through my head.
>
> All this took several hours, and, by now, the first section was far down the valley and the next could be heard behind it and the third was well down below me. I heard the Germans down below calling, "Hi, Tommy, come here", and some soldiers shouted as they were captured arriving down at the road below. I was quite prepared to believe these were my own patrol. Every time there was anything like a good haul, the donkey brayed like some animal in distress, but rather mechanical. I knew this now to be their success signal.
>
> I ventured to move to a more comfortable position and fell to sleep. I woke with what seemed like something lightly tapping my

leg, but I could see nothing. I was very thirsty, very, very hungry and I remembered I had had nothing to eat for twenty-four hours, and then a very scratch breakfast.

I noticed some sheep grazing above me and one, in particular, seemed to be watching me. I was now in full light of the moon. I resolved, come what may, I would not be frightened of sheep. Perhaps I was a little mad by this time, as I quite distinctly remember asking the sheep if it would like to take me prisoner before I moved off. The poor ewe seemed interested but did not take me prisoner!

It was now about 4 o'clock in the morning and I resolved not to worry about my things until later on, when I would come back in the daylight and pick them up. I now made my way across the valley and round the hill to the R.V. I had never been to the R.V. this way before and it was much farther than I had thought. To make matters worse, before I got there I ran into a German patrol. I saw them quite distinctly in the bush and they must have seen me, for I had appeared on the skyline. I found a very good rock crevice, however, and got down in this, well-hidden, as I thought. Something, however, found me and I now think it must have been a dog, for I certainly felt it sniff my leg, and when I looked up, there was nothing, only the sound of light padded feet running away. At the time I was almost convinced that it was sheep, but I saw nothing. Now, for the next part of my story, there will, no doubt, be those who will say that I was out of my mind – we know that the human mind can imagine almost anything. There will be others who will call it a miracle. But call it what you will, here is the story. I said a prayer to God to protect me from these creatures of Hitler and to see me safely back to Cairo by Christmas. Remember, I had faith and I believe, greater than a grain of mustard seed.

I got up and walked on. I then found that the mule, which had been on the other side of the hill early in the night, was now just below me. I might have considered that there were Germans nearby, but I was beyond caring now and it was getting daylight. My thirst was driving me on, as I knew there was water in this valley where

> we had hidden it, so I made for that. I walked around, up and down valleys for some time, unable to find it and I remembered Corporal Rupping had said that one would not find it unless one knew where to look. I did not know where to look.
>
> I wandered round that valley for some time, until I began to believe I was in the wrong valley, so I made up for where we had camped the night after the first day's battle. I found this without trouble but could find no water anywhere about, nor any boxes of rations, or anything else, although there were certainly a lot of old tins. Now, I decided to go back to the river where B. Squadron H.Q. had been and there, I should certainly find some water down the river.

Before long, Olivey was distracted by a mule, probably the same as that seen earlier. Observing its progress in the hilly terrain, he decided this was a sign for him to go up or downhill, according to the mule's movements. The behaviour of birds were obviously another indicator, the direction and tone of their chirping providing further clues as to how and where Olivey should proceed. But wherever he went, he found only abandoned hiding places and the detritus of war.

> I heard talking. Somewhere a dog barked. Ah, a dog. What did that mean? Danger, no doubt. My birds were waking up again. I got up and they led me on down into another river. I still found no water, however, and by now I was getting desperate. I sat down again, although the birds were most insistent I should go on. I moved on a little farther and lay down in another hideout in the river bed. Still there was no water. I stopped to think – Oh, God, what did all this mean? I prayed that I might understand it all, as I believed by this time some German organisation had got hold of me.

Olivey raged at the Germans and in his delirium was sure he heard the voice of his father telling his mother to talk to their son. He closed his eyes and felt his mother take his hand in hers, as she assured him that everything would be all right.

I asked her, was I dead? Both my mother and father had been dead for some years. She answered, no, but I would understand it all in time, that I must not worry, God was in his heaven and all was well with the world. I asked, might I see God? She answered, yes, but now I must keep quiet and all these things would be explained to me. I asked her, should I escape from the Germans? She said, yes, but I must not worry, it would all be explained to me in time, but now I must go to sleep. I said I wanted water. She told me it was up in the Italian barracks, but if I went up there I should find some nasty German policemen. I laughed at her expression, which had been the one we used in my childhood. I asked her, could I go back to my wife? She said I could do anything if I had faith. So I told her I had faith, but didn't understand, would she explain? She said, yes, it would all be explained to me, but now I must go to sleep, as she must return to daddy. I asked, where was daddy and she answered, with God. Then might I see God? Yes, but not yet, she replied. I asked her, did she love me, and she answered, of course, and she asked me, did I love her, and I answered, what did she think? Which was the opposite way to the procedure in my childhood after I had had a nightmare, and always ended with a kiss, but now we both laughed and she was gone.

CHAPTER 12

Capture

Driven by his thirst, and also encouraged by his perceived encounter with his long-dead mother, Olivey decided to risk returning to the Italian barracks at Clidi.

> I slowly found my way up the river and arrived via the road at the Italian barracks. All the way up I had been thinking to myself, I'm going to find breakfast in the barracks, I know, because I have faith. I seem to have lost my thirst but was looking forward to some tea. Yes, I had faith and I would be in Cairo for Christmas and with my wife. Everything was possible with faith, but now I was looking forward to bacon and eggs, but, as my mother had said, I should learn.
>
> I looked in the room of the barracks, but there was no one there. I looked in last of all at the Italian commandant's dining room, at a great big pot of bacon dripping. I looked in the cupboard at bread and a bottle of wine. Oh, good, oh, good. I sat down and ate. Certainly, the bread was mouldy in places, but the dripping was good and I filled myself with bread and dripping. The wine was very dry, almost sour, but I could find no water. It was now about 8 o'clock and there was no one about. I looked in 2nd Lieutenant Pizzigoni's bedroom and found a bed with sheets and blankets, very clean. First, I took from my wallet four or five Italian 1,000 lire notes and put these in an envelope addressed to some poor Greek who thoughtfully had left the dripping, and a note under a jagged piece of bomb saying that poor M— had been killed by German bombs. These Greek inhabitants had most certainly suffered badly and I was bound to feel that perhaps we were in part to blame.

> I next went into the bedroom, and here found a beaker of water. Having closed the shutters so I could still see out, I undressed and slipped in between the sheets, knowing that, as a light sleeper, I should wake if anyone arrived. I passed straight out without a thought.

When Olivey awoke, it was mid-afternoon. As he was gathering his thoughts, the door opened and five Germans entered the room. There were clearly surprised to find the building occupied.

> The junior officer spoke perfect English, and, coming in, asked what I was doing there. Before waiting for a reply, he spotted my battledress coat with the three pips, hanging over a chair. He was obviously very pleased with his capture. I sat up and said, "Good afternoon. Very good game we have had – quite enjoyed it myself. Hope you weren't hurt yourself." He thought this a very good joke and told everybody. I then spoke German, but I found my German had much deteriorated since last night and he said, "You speak Afrikaans and German mixed." I told him I was a South African and gave him my rank, name and number on a piece of paper. As L.R.D.G. shoulder titles were still on my battledress, I said I was L.R.D.G. He remarked that he had noticed that – and my M.C. ribbon. He congratulated me. By this time, I was dressed. He asked if there was any water about. I showed him the beaker on the dressing table. He was about to pour it out when I told him I would like to drink it.
>
> I then told him I had left my revolver up the road and requested we should fetch it. We walked up the road, the other officer and I. He spoke very little English. My object in going up was to retrieve my kit, especially my cigarette case. I knew there was the sniper's rifle there, which I would give him. As we got down the valley, I suppose the same idea struck him, as it did me, that I could make a break for it now. I had been limping, but there was nothing wrong with my foot. Should I do it, I realised, I should not get far, and, in any case, I was resigned to my fate by now.
>
> He said, "Come, we return", and so near my kit I had to go back. There, Jerries had arrived in a jeep and trailer. Their first

objective was to collect all water and I afterwards discovered that this was their plan throughout the island, thus forcing troops to give themselves up. They also placed guards on all wells. I noticed it was not an L.R.D.G. jeep. They were some party of salvage corps. They had collected anything of any use, including the dripping. I also noticed the Germans opened my envelope and pocketed the money. The piece of bomb they threw outside. It was useless to protest and I wished him bad luck with the money in my thoughts, and I have no doubt it has done him no good. We now drove down the road and back to what used to be Navy House in the centre of the island. Here, they had collected and piled up Bren guns, rifles and numerous other things. I noticed with satisfaction that only about 10% of the weapons were still serviceable. The officers went into the house with the dripping. I remained in the car. One of the German soldiers came up to me and asked me to show him how to take the sling off a rifle. I noticed the rifle had no bolt. I went and took a good rifle with a bolt on it, and having removed the bolt, put it in my pocket. I then showed him how simple it was to take off the sling when you know how. He still hadn't got the hang of it, so I took another rifle, again removing the bolt, and showed him again. He then took a rifle, removed the bolt, which I took, and after some difficulty got the sling off. The officers appeared, everyone stood to attention, and I got in the jeep. I had charged him three bolts for his lesson – I was able to throw them away later on. I was taken to the town hall and told to wait in the jeep while the officer went in and reported my capture. When he came out, he told me I should now report to the commandant. I shook hands, promised to see him in Berlin after the war, gave him an excellent salute and he drove off. The Germans' saluting was very good. Everybody salutes everybody in the German army, especially if you have a prisoner with you, and the Jerries love it. We had talked of many things in the short time we were together and he had said that they could not understand why we had surrendered so soon. I told him that up to the time we surrendered, their casualties had been heavier than ours. Immediately this position altered, there was no point in us fighting on. We knew from the start we could not hold the island without air cover and most of the best troops had been taken off the island the night before last. We should now be better employed eating German food, than as dead men. He considered the end of the war would be in April. He did not say who would win, though I thought this was pretty obvious.

I now turned about to go in and report to the commandant. As I was about to enter the building, I was greeted by two British officers. One said, "Oh, L.R.D.G.? New sort of position for you to be in, isn't it?" I thought he sounded rather jeering, so I replied, "Oh, we often find ourselves in this position temporarily, but don't worry, just have faith my friends!" I then went upstairs and found myself with a whole crowd of soldiers: English, Irish, Indians. I sat down and had a smoke with them. They all seemed quite happy, though they complained they had had no food and the place was filthy dirty. I then went and had a wash. The Germans were obviously very frightened that our Navy would come and sink their landing craft and everyone was busy packing up to get away as soon as possible back to [---].

I think it was while I was washing that a German soldier came round asking if there were any officers there, as they were being taken down to the docks. My coat was off so I made no indication that I was an officer, and having had my wash, I went back to the soldiers and told them that from now on, my name was John and I was a private soldier like themselves. It was still rather difficult for them not to call me 'Sir'. I suppose it is something to do with the way one speaks, because although few of the troops recognised me from now on, it was not long before I had the nickname of 'The Toff'.

I had a tin of emergency ration chocolate which I donated and so made a good brew of cocoa which was just ready when the order came for everyone to go downstairs. So foolish are the soldiers that most of them left the cocoa and went. I stayed and drank mine and afterwards filled my water bottle and a spare bottle with this most welcome liquid. I thought I had been left behind but a German soldier came up, and, ordering me to give up my watch, which I refused to do, told me he was going to the commandant.

An N.C.O. came up and ordered me down. Like a fool, perhaps, I told him the soldier had tried to steal my wristwatch. He gave the soldier hell, but I had to go down. I kept my watch, however, which I now put in my pocket.

I seemed to have collected quite a bit of kit in the place for I now had a water bottle, a haversack, a towel, some soap, a mug, knife and fork. I had taken off my cap badge, shoulder titles, pips, M.C. ribbon and had developed a West Country accent.

We were issued a tin of Italian bully beef. I managed to get three tins, as I was the last! We now fell in and were marched off under a British sergeant and a Jerry soldier. I was all ready to slip away into one of the houses but the sergeant had become very pro-German and when I endeavoured to slip into one of the houses in the village, he came and pulled me out. I told him he was due for a court-martial, as no one else had seen me go, the Jerry marching in front leading the way. I never got his name or I certainly would report him.

I was watched from now on and no other chance occurred. The Tommies all threw away their tins hats and eventually we arrived at the docks, singing "It's a long way to Tipperary". The Italians were having a service and someone was preaching a sermon. The docks were filled with prisoners.

I found out where the L.R.D.G. chaps were and I waited until dark.

At dark I wandered up to them and as I was recognised the party gave a shout of welcome. I pointed to my lack of pips and told them to keep quiet. I asked who else was there and heard that Dick Lawson was with the officers. I asked someone to get hold of him for me if they could. I ordered everyone to take off their cap badges and shoulder titles as the L.R.D.G. were sure to be specially picked out, and if anyone wanted to get away, it would be hopeless. I then exchanged battledress coats with someone, as mine still showed where the pips had been. I got a very good one in exchange. Mine, I fear, was rather dirty. Dick turned up and we sat down on the quay and talked. He told me most of the news, how Alan and Jake had met their end.

No doubt, the two officers also swopped tales about how they had been captured. Lawson had also attempted to get away from the island. On learning that Brigadier Tilney had surrendered, he had taken charge of a party of about twenty personnel of the LRDG and made his way towards Patella and the nearby Battery Ducci at the entrance to Portolago. He was soon joined by other stragglers. At dawn on 17 November a large caique arrived:

'Although none of us believed it was English there was a general movement and about 120 people appeared from bushes and rocks like the dead rising. There was nothing, having decided to stay with the party since I started it, but to go and I went to the shore where they put water off from the boat and said they would take us off at 12. However, some more Jerries appeared from above and we were taken back to Ducci Battery where we washed and made a stew from what the Italians had left and later marched into Portolago.'

Olivey confided in his friend that he was still intent on escaping.

> I told him that I intended to get away at the first opportunity and he said he thought there would be more chance in Greece. I told him I should not mix with the L.R.D.G. much from now on and was now a member of 1st Sherwood Foresters, which, after all, was correct.
>
> I went and slept with some others in a small space I found in the middle of the docks. I had no blanket or coat and was feeling rather lonely in all this crowd of soldiers, all talking of their experiences and finding lost friends. I remembered suddenly how Jake had once said that often when he did not know quite what to do, he would think of some special friend, whom he respected for his judgement and sincerity, and would think what would he have done in such a case? Jake himself was one of these people who seemed to do the right thing and whose lead one could follow. I made a fire and started to heat up a tin of bully. I was now joined by about half a dozen chaps and soon we had quite a jolly party. One sergeant of the Buffs was most amusing and I took to him at once.

The general trend of conversation was a grouse that the promised air cover had not been forthcoming and that they had been promised they would never have to fight again without air cover after Dunkirk.

Much laughter was caused by stories of lone battles which were fought after the island had surrendered by men who had received no orders to give up. It was all rather fine to hear these men talking again, almost as though they had won the battle and it certainly cheered one up to know that the Empire still held such fine types. One often heard that the [---] officers had never given an order from beginning to end of the [---] show and no one knew what they were supposed to do. One man related how they had put out to sea the night before on a caique to go to Turkey, how they had met a destroyer which everyone took to be British. When they got on board however, they found it was a German ship, which brought them round here as prisoners. I remembered the destroyer I had seen. We talked until midnight, after which I got a couple of hours sleep.

I woke up early and wandered round. The German guard had got a bit tipsy on wine or rum and one German soldier, speaking English, was holding forth at great length.

At daybreak the Italians were going out to get water at the well outside the enclosure. I went out with them and filled my water bottle. Then, pretending I was looking for something to put more water in, I slipped away out of camp. I walked boldly up the road. There seemed to be no one about. My birds were singing again. This was obviously the way to go. I walked on and on till I came to a cottage just below our old L.R.D.G. Q stores and here I found two women drawing water at a well. I felt thirsty, so I sat down, and having drunk, I helped them carry the water tins up to the house. They were almost in tears and would have had me stop, why I didn't, I can't think, except that I was keen on getting back to the area of 320 and Z-barges. I gave them a W/T set I found in the [roadside] ditch and asked them to hide it. This they did. I made a sign of the cross to show them I wished them God's blessing and went on my way. A dog was barking so I knew there was danger ahead but

I kept on and picked up a tin of peas in the ditch. Some German soldiers now came down the road to see what I was doing. I showed them the tin of peas and said I had nothing to eat, no blankets, and the commandant had told me to come up here and re-equip myself. I helped them carry boxes of fruit up to their house. Chiefly they wanted vegetables. They seemed to be very hungry for these and there were none in the rations. These German quartermasters or storemen did not seem over interested in the war and were simply out to collect as much to eat as possible. They had already caught three chickens of the Greeks and these were plucked and ready for cooking. I got a complete kit together at this dump. Razor, vest, pants, mug, knife, spoon, fork, cap comforter, which I now wore in place of my beret, several slabs of chocolate, a tin of milk, a tin of peaches, a water bottle full of rum, three warm American blankets and a strap to hold these together, spare socks – I could find no boots. While I was here, they produced three telescopes which had belonged to us. They could not make them work and I, putting them just out of focus, showed them they were useless. I showed, however, how useful the lenses were to make glasses to light cigarettes with and there was a mad rush to pull them to pieces to get a glass each. So, they had ruined three perfectly good telescopes for us. They wanted to take me all over the dump to find vegetables but I said there were none, which, in any case, I believe was true, so, pocketing a few packets of cigarettes, off I went with many "Auf Wiedersehens" and promises to meet in Berlin.

I went on down the road and there met a party marching back – the corporal wanted to know where I was going. I said to the hospital. He said that was good!

I now turned off the road, as I hoped to skirt along the coast to the bay in the north. I had not got far, however, when, at a cottage, the Greeks told me there were Germans in the trees. I then heard firing – they were looking for an escaped English officer I was told. They came out and we started talking. They would have it that I was an officer but I persuaded them that I was not and that I was going to the hospital to see if I could find my little brother who had been wounded and that I must be able to tell my mother that I had

> seen him after the battle if he was alive. It seemed a good story and would have had the sympathy, I felt, of any British soldier, but, I fear, had little effect on the Germans. I was taken to Navy House and I hoped that the German officer was no longer there, although I doubt if he would have recognised me, now I had shaved and changed a bit.
>
> I spent an hour waiting for him, and as he did not turn up, asked if I might have a sleep under the trees. At first this was refused, but afterwards I was allowed. Now, this was necessary as I wished to destroy my officer's pass which I knew was in my wallet. Having destroyed this, I had a sleep. Some German soldier was produced who I had never seen before and he declared I was the missing officer. No doubt he had lost one and was glad to produce another. I thanked them all very much for the promotion and suggested lunch. I now pulled their legs about Russia and Germany and drew a large map of Europe to show where my home was. This map made Germany very small and Russia extended over two tables. They saw the point of it and thought it very funny. They now allowed me to go and see my brother in hospital. The only L.R.D.G. I found there was Signalman du Toit but I told him he was now my brother and we talked for a while. I was then marched back with a party from the hospital to the docks.

Lance Corporal Hendrik P. du Toit later made an unsuccessful attempt to escape. Due to his wounds becoming infected, he was forced to return to hospital.

> We found that the prisoners had been moved to the area of the seaplane base and were now in two large buildings there. I was just in time to draw the daily ration of macaroni which, half cooked and consisting of about four spoonful's, was our daily ration of food. I drank some water out of a well. It was not drinking water, but what matter? I now found a party of L.R.D.G. and went and had a chat.
>
> I spent the night on a table and again woke early. Everything was very quiet but one German came in and spoke to another. He

said, "We are all leaving on the ship." Then they both went out. I lay and thought about this for a long time and I imagined that all the Jerries were leaving from the island. Was it possible a counter-attack was being put on? And I remembered how frightened the Jerries had been of losing their shipping in the harbour and in the bay at night and the feverish haste of everyone.

I got up just before dawn and went out to see if the guard had gone, but I had a great disappointment as two Germans were still sitting huddled up in their greatcoats with rifles. I asked them where the others were going, but they were sullen and wouldn't talk.

At sunrise, I left my kit with a party of Irishmen who were brewing some tea round a fire, and taking my water bottle, boldly walked out of the gate. The sentry wanted to know where I was going. I told him for water. I did not walk towards the water, however, pretending to have lost my way. The sentry started shouting, "Hi! Ah! You! Stupid!" I took no notice and pretended not to hear. I heard him rattle his bolt, but by this time I was fairly well away, and, turning right, disappeared behind a building. There were now great shouts and one soldier came running after me. In Hitler's circus, like every other circus, the farther you get away from the men who actually perform in the centre of the ring, the more foolish people you meet. The artist himself who does the fighting is usually the best type. The others are a gutless crowd, afraid of themselves, some of them. This soldier was no exception and when he came running up to me with his rifle, I could see he hadn't enough faith in himself to shoot. I told him I was looking for a tin to put some water in. He said no, I must return, and took me by the coat sleeve. I looked at him molesting me and then at him, as much as to say, how dare you touch me? I had an idea that his military law would be a bit hazy. He immediately let go and started to beg me to come back with him. I told him I should look for a tin and then return. He pleaded some more but he saw it was to no avail. He then ran off back again and I moved into a house that I noticed up the hill and very close to the wire fence which ran round the place. The house had obviously been used by the Italians as a store for seaplane kit and had a number of boxes of parachute flares and explosives of various kinds. I took a fairly big box and put it up against the door of one of the small rooms in such a way as to make it appear as though it had been put there from the outside. I then sat down and waited. First, I heard shouts and then an odd shot or two and then a burst of sub-machine-gun fire. Chaps came all round the home and one came inside but went away without looking in my room. This lasted for about an hour and then everything settled down peacefully.

I thought to myself, if I can remain here three days or so, I shall miss the boat which will take the prisoners off and shall then be able to slip away and over to Turkey. I began to plan which route I should go and had everything cut and dried. For something to do, I then started to collect a few cards together which I thought might amuse my friends as Christmas cards. They had been sent to some Italian airman who must have been stationed in this house. I collected one for everyone and started to put them in order as I thought them more suitable for the various people. In this sort of way: I chose a card and thought of a friend, then I would look to see what there was on the card which would make me think of this friend. I had in my hand a card, which may have been an Easter card, as there was a big egg and a lady (very Italian!) looking at a lamb. She wore evening dress and was sitting on her ostrich feather fan. I thought of P. B., an old friend of mine. I could not see anything to remind me of her in the card, and I thought to remind me of her and Christmas, there must be a 'ham bone' somewhere – a little joke we had had in my youth. But look as I would, I could see none, even on the sheep, unless, of course, the lady was sitting on it. This made me laugh and I knew then it was meant for P., as she had always made me laugh.

I don't think I made any noise but I had only been in the room about four hours when some German soldier decided to look in the room, and there I was caught. Like all Jerries, on seeing me, he closed the door and went away and came back brandishing an automatic. I had to go. I was taken before the commandant who wanted to know how I got there and what I was doing. And why I had put the box against the door.

I replied that some of his soldiers had taken me there as I wished to write. They had closed me in. This shook the old man that his soldiers could be so disloyal! I told him I was an author and was trying to find somewhere peaceful. He took the list of Christmas cards I had made out and hoped, I suppose, to find something of national interest. I was told to stay inside. I tried then to find the Irishman who had my kit but could find him nowhere and so lost my kit. With it, all my extra food and a bottle of rum. I never found it again, though I heard some Irishmen having a party that evening.

I found some L.R.D.G. chaps and shared some food with them on top of a house. Dick had taken a party to bury Jake and they did not return until dark. They had, after burying Jake, gone to see a South African who was fighting for the Germans. He had taken them to a dump and they, in exchange for sharing with him a can of milk, had loaded themselves with provisions. I joined their party, which consisted of Sergeant J. [Sydney Jenkinson], Corporal W. [William F. Whitehead], Lance Corporal G. [sic: Alfred I. Curle], Signalman [H. J.] Evershed. We parked down on the roof of the building and had a good feed.

During the night, some Jerry came up asking for L.R.D.G. They wanted one, so the troops sent him over to us. I woke up thinking they were looking for me and hoped one of the others would own up. But they were more awake than I and none of them were L.R.D.G. The Jerry went off in tears almost. I noticed that of all the prisoners, L.R.D.G. chaps were by far the best provisioned and this was simply because we had taken the trouble to go out and get stuff from the dumps. I fear we were rather the envy of the other troops. Curle, for example, had so much stuff that he could hardly carry it. I was travelling light, but, of course, had to carry my share of the foodstuff. First thing in the morning we were told to pack up as we were moving. Most of the troops immediately made a rush to get [there] first. We sat down and cooked our breakfast. Now, if there is one thing we had all learnt, it was always to be nearly last on a boat – not quite last if you could time it, because then, besides getting a good position, you were more likely to be on deck. Sure enough, we timed it beautifully and all had seats on the hatch, where others were in the hold or on the deck. The ship, which was about a 6,000 tonner, was crowded with men, all British troops and officers. I cannot congratulate the officers on looking after their men, for with the exception of Dick Lawson and the English Church Padre, no officer took any interest in the men's welfare at all. Dick and the Padre were excellent and between them organised everything.

Olivey was among some 2,700 prisoners of war to board *Catherine Schiaffino* on 20 November for passage to the mainland. The steamship left Portolago the same day, together with two warships transporting German combat troops from Leros.

The sergeants and sergeant majors, with few exceptions, had all been taken away on a boat the day before as an advance party, but I suppose this was done so we should not get organised, and it certainly worked. No one amongst a lot of soldiers is going to be the first to move and I fancy we should have had no food had the two officers [mentioned] above not looked after our interest.

They worked hard and we received an issue of biscuits and cheese for the trip. Our knives had been taken from us but most chaps still had clasp knives to open tins of bully. Our party made a biscuit tin full of coffee, steam was available, again thanks to Dick and the Padre. The night was cold and we were glad of our blankets. We were obviously making for Athens. I had a compass and was able to follow the direction, more or less. In the convoy were two destroyers, which followed us. During the hours on the boat, I had time to reflect on my own position and it became immediately obvious to me that if I was going to stay with the troops throughout my time in prison, I was in for a very rough time, not only because I should have to work, because I am fond of work as a means of passing the time, but also because I should not be accepted by the private soldier. I am not a snob, but somehow or other, I suppose never having mixed enough with the lower classes, I find they are very hard to understand. One offers friendship and at once it is rejected. They seem to consider that because one ventures and sometimes gains, that is on account of being a 'toff', and not because one has ventured and it is the reward of endeavour. They resent success as though it were a personal crime. I had asked my next-door neighbour to call me by my Christian name and not keep calling me Sir. From then on, I was blessed with hearing my name shouted by this otherwise normal individual on all occasions, as though I were his best friend and I remembered how I had stopped this when serving in the ranks before. I remembered how, in desperation, I had lived a life apart when in the ranks because I could not stick their endless talk of women and impossible happenings. This had been four years ago and I was not at all certain I could stick it again after three years in the Officers' Mess. On the other hand, I like the comradeship of the ranks, and there were times when I felt that this was certainly the best position in the army, with no cares or responsibilities.

The troops, I found, talked themselves into things so easily and I was already being talked into the impossibility of escaping. Even my L.R.D.G. chaps were saying it was impossible – all except Whitehead, who cheered me up more than he knew.

No, I determined that at the first taking of names I would make myself known. I would then have plenty of excuses as, after all, no one had yet asked for it. If I had not mixed with the officers, it was because I didn't know any of them, except the doctor, who might be staying with the troops. This was not quite true, as I noticed Lieutenant F. [Freeman?] and Captain Dudley Folland in the officers' crowd. The remainder had been taken by air I presumed.

We ran up the estuary to Athens the next day at about 10 a.m. Here, I fell in for a fatigue with three other chaps. I was told to wash the side of the ship. There had been no latrine on board and the side of the ship had been used, with results that can be imagined.

Still, I never had to wash the ship because as fast as the sailor turned on the water at the stopcocks, we turned it off further back and when the water did arrive eventually, the hose was leading into the engine room, so they turned it off down there! We reported to the major who had given us the job that there was no water available and fell out.

We pulled into Piraeus Harbour at about noon. I could not help thinking what a wonderful chance this would have been to blow the side of the ship had I some plastic [explosive] and a time pencil. Everyone could have been off the ship before it sank. One cannot foresee these things, however.

We formed up in fives by five and were so counted into a line of march. Now, this was the first time they had taken a check of how many prisoners there were. I estimated that there were about 1,500–2,000, but it was difficult to say. None of my own patrol were present and I began to wonder if they had all got away or been kept separate from the remainder. Was it possible that those soldiers who had had contact with the sheep hunting platoon had been kept separate on purpose?

Of those who were at Clidi, Rifleman Oelofse was dead; Signalman Todman, wounded on 14 November, would die in hospital and Signalman Bremner was wounded and a prisoner of war. During the battle, X2 Patrol, it will be remembered, had been joined by several New Zealanders. At least three are thought to have been among those who were later evacuated from Leros. Seven of X2 Patrol were also taken prisoner. Years later, Rhodesian, Gordon R. 'Brick' Broderick, recalled the withdrawal from Battery Ciano and his decision to surrender:

'I buried my "Oom Paul" sovereign [Krugerrand], which had been through both the Boer War and the Great War before me, together with the bolt of my rifle on the slopes of Mount Clidi. By a roundabout route, it took until evening to regroup, but Olivey was not there and we dispersed to meet again the next evening. Mortar shells were fired into the hills during the day to try and flush out any remnants of the defenders. This made the wait nerve-racking. John Olivey was still absent that evening as we shared our rations before waiting another day. That evening we discovered that some shepherds had found our ration cache and made off with the remaining food and water. Lemmer [Rifleman R. N. Lemmer], McLeod [Rifleman Robert I. Mcleod], Malan [Rifleman Peter S. S. Malan], Winter [Acting Corporal Peter

Winter] and I gave our remaining rations to those who had elected to try and escape and we gave ourselves up to a German sentry lower down the hill. He directed us to what had been our forward dressing station, still manned by British medics. It was there that I saw Toddy for the last time. He gave me a wan smile and then died. A senior German officer called us together and told us that he was pleased to be talking to such fine soldiers and thanked us for a good, clean fight!! He then instructed us to follow the path down to Alinda Bay Hospital and to remain as a group of disciplined men.'

Olivey would not learn of the fate of his men until much later, however.

> It took about two hours to get off the ship and formed up. We had enjoyed pulling the leg of the Prussian commandant who, every time someone would put his hand up to scratch his head on passing him, would return a salute. He got furious every time he was caught and he could see we were laughing at him. He was a typical Prussian, as depicted in all the books, going grey and obviously of the last war. The cameras had been busy trying to get photos but all they got was the Churchill 'V' sign, which they didn't want. There was now quite a large crowd collected at the dock gates and along the railings and the chaps started singing "It's a long way to Tipperary" and other songs. The crowd got quite enthusiastic and had to be dispersed by the Germans. Our guards caused us a great deal of amusement. They were old men, most of them, and looked as though they had been put into uniform for the occasion. They had no military bearing at all and had no idea how to carry their rifles. Their field grey uniforms were obviously just out of store and still had the creases where they had been folded – they fitted where they touched! One old Pole who was standing opposite us had buttoned up his tunic having missed the top button. He could not make out what was wrong until we pointed it out to him. He was most ashamed. All of us could speak a little German and we kept on pulling their legs unmercifully, telling them the Russians were now in Poland, to which they replied "*Gut*".

One soldier was only a boy of about sixteen. Whitehead offered to carry his rifle for him, as this was obviously too heavy for him. He nearly cried and I'm sure tears came to his eyes when we told him to go back to [---]. It was all very amusing and the troops were having a grand time. Everyone was shouting "*Funf! Funf!*", which meant we were to stay in our fives. Orders came through that we were to march in a soldier-like manner and on no account were to cause a disturbance amongst the Greeks who would only suffer. There was to be no singing as we marched through the town. As soon as we set off it became obvious that it was quite impossible to march in any sort of step without music or anyone shouting the step and it was only more or less possible to keep in one's '*Funf*' by dint of pushing those with large loads and sometimes passing them, [leaving them] to struggle on behind. We must have looked a most untidy mob. We gathered we had about 10 miles to march. I settled down to enjoy it, and not having much to carry except my blankets slung around me, my haversack on my back and my water bottle. My rations were in my haversack. The Greek people were marvellous. They obviously could not show much of their feelings, as they had been warned that demonstrations would be severely dealt with.

Many of the older women were weeping and we spoke words of encouragement to them such as, "Cheer up, mumma". Men would stand on the side of the road and give us a large wink behind the Germans' backs. Girls were waving from the houses. Occasionally, someone would throw a packet of cigarettes. The Jerries would try to intercept these, and if they succeeded, all the troops around would growl their disapproval. The Jerry would look cross and everyone would sneer. They soon found they could not do just as they pleased with us. Despite orders, there were occasional songs in the ranks. No one was worrying very much and rather enjoying the fun. It was certainly deteriorating into a victory march as far as Jerry was concerned.

CHAPTER 13

Escape and Evasion

Together with other LRDG whom he had joined at Portolago, Olivey continued marching east towards Athens.

> A truck continually passed up and down the line, supposed to be taking pictures for the press and the cinema, but every time it came near, we would pass the word up the line and everyone would give the 'V' sign and look happy. It was fast getting dusk as we had started late, so that before we reached Athens' streets, it was dark. The shops were lit. We passed a large hotel where German women in uniform were sitting with their officer friends. Someone said, "Ah, German WAAS's", and everyone laughed, much to their annoyance, as they felt we were laughing at them.

WAAS may be an erroneous reference to the South African Women's Auxiliary Service (SAWAS), formed early in the Second World War for maintaining the good morale of servicemen and women.

> The streets were crowded and people would look in our faces and ask if we were English. We told them yes. Many, however, took us for Italians.

For the Greeks, life under German occupation was no laughing matter, and the seemingly endless procession of defeated but still cheerful British soldiers was incomprehensible and a depressing spectacle. One hardly ever sees happy, smiling faces in newsreels of American, Russian, and especially German, vanquished. Such behaviour is peculiar to the British.

There were some, of course, who were determined not to spend the rest of the war in captivity. But these were a minority. Most, it seems, were of the opinion that it was simply too dangerous for any escape attempt. Their pessimism was affecting Olivey. He began to lose heart, knowing that the longer he delayed, the less chance there was that he would ever get away.

At dusk, the column left the built-up area of Athens and passed through more open terrain. Olivey considered his chances. Somewhere, a dog barked. Olivey hesitated, taking this a sign, a warning that he should wait. Meanwhile, the prisoners were beginning to straggle, obliging their guards to widen their spacing. Initially, one soldier had been posted alongside every fifth row, or so. Soon, they were about 20 yards apart. Olivey whispered to Sergeant Jenkinson, 'This is where I get off.' Jenkinson wished him luck. At a bend in the road, a side lane came into view and Olivey made his move.

> There were some people standing, watching us pass. Very few of them saw me clear down that lane. I was gone in a flash and shot into the first house I saw. I don't suppose the Germans ever missed me, except that there were no longer '*Funf*' in our '*Funf*'. I got down under a table and waited. Two Greek women came in the yard. They had seen me go. They asked if I was English and I said, yes, English. They both kissed me. I was given an overcoat and taken to another house very quickly. On entering the house, I made the sign of the cross and thanked God.
>
> What wonderful people I had struck. The family consisted of the father, a short little man, sturdily built; the mother, a medium light woman, rather on the thin side. Both were about 40 or 45 years old. A little son, typical of all Greek boys, aged about 10, a little girl of about 8 and her sister about 6. I was at once given a suit of clothes to put on and my uniform put out of sight. The home consisted of this one room about 15 feet square. The family were at supper. I had, of course, kissed the two little girls, and they were both holding my hands and very pleased with their capture. I was now invited to sit down and have some supper and everyone

gave up a portion of their rissole for me. Certainly there is no generosity like the poor's. I told my story and that I was an English officer. It seemed that the lady herself was a British subject, having been born in Malta. She still had her British passport.

It was difficult to talk, as we had no common language, and I at once noticed they were very suspicious of any German I spoke. This was natural in a land where Gestapo abound. I learnt that a German soldier lived in each of the houses on each side of this one, but I should be quite safe here for the night. In the morning, they would take me to another place. I was given the little boy's bed, and the three children climbed into one bed, while father and mother occupied the third bed. I was very tired, and after producing all my kit, I got into bed. I had been carrying a first aid kit haversack when I got away and on opening this, I found several articles which would be of use to the mother, also a box of potato chips. I had three tins of bully beef and two tins of carrots in my haversack. I, who, like the early Christians, had started off with nothing, but now had sufficient for my needs. Everyone spoke in whispers, I noticed, and supposed that the bullying Germans had so frightened these poor people that they hardly dared to open their mouths.

We were all soon asleep and I, especially, slept the sleep of the just. We woke at sunrise and quickly dressed. I think I shall always remember that suit of clothes I was given – the trousers, a leather brown colour, had seen many summers, I fancy, and had been patched with blue material at the knees and seat. They were far too short for me, but by pulling them down, they had looked alright. My shirt had been given to me by a friend of my host who had happened to come in, and, seeing my needs, had at once given me his shirt, coat and tie. The coat was quite a good fit, a bit short in the arms perhaps, with also a patch of blue at the elbows. But an overcoat of dark material, much worn at the collar and cuffs, covered the coat and made me feel fit for the road. I had no hat but then I had already noticed that nearly all the men and certainly all the women wore no hats, so there was nothing strange in this. I had forgotten to change my shoes and still had on the slippers when we started off, so had to return immediately and put on my own brown shoes. We walked back along the road I had come and into Athens' streets again. There were not many people about and my host, looking at me, nodded his approval. That I looked Greek enough I felt sure, except for my English face and blue eyes.

We came after about a mile to some Italian soldiers sitting outside some large building and here my host obtained a key from a friend. This opened a door which led down into a cellar close by and here was a shop. I at once felt I should be able to help the good man, as I am useful at odd jobs like that.

The shop belonged to a tinsmith, referred to hereon as Costas (the same pseudonym is provided for his young son). While in Athens, Olivey knew most people only by their first name. He, in turn, was usually introduced as 'Mr John'.

Another man came in and we shook hands. The rubbing of the two index fingers of both hands together indicated that they were fast friends. I sat in this cellar all day. No one came to the shop and any trade was done at the door. The little son, Costas, arrived about 10 o'clock and seemed to be the principal workman. He was left in charge of the shop while my host disappeared.

It seems he had gone to the Greek Consulate or Red Cross and had tried to obtain a pass for me. Everyone carries a pass in Greece with a photo and particulars of himself. I was not surprised to hear they were issuing no more passes.

My lunch was obtained from a shop round the corner and consisted of a tin of baked beans – very good, for I was hungry – also some brown bread. It seems that bread is rationed but there is an active black market in Greece from which one can obtain anything if one is prepared to pay. I knew my host was poor and felt ashamed at accepting this hospitality, but felt I should not be there long, so it would not matter. At night, another tin of baked beans and bread was produced, the cellar was closed up, and a bed made up for me in the corner. I remained here all night. This was my life for a week, except I asked for a dictionary so I could make myself understood. A pocket Greek-English dialogue book was produced and from this I would sort out a sentence and point to the Greek equivalent. In this way, I indicated I should like to speak to an English-speaking person, if one was procurable. In the evening, a lady came to see me. I asked her to tell my host that I would like him to get in touch with the English Mission, which I knew existed to help escaping prisoners of war. He said he would try, but that there were many spies and Gestapo speaking English and it was difficult. Still, I had got something moving. One day a Boy Scout, who also spoke quite good English, visited me and later brought me a map of Greece, a hat and a compass. I, of course, had a compass but it was good of him to think of it. He was an excellent youngster and filled me with hope. Perhaps after a week in this cellar, I was showing a bit of restlessness, for my host came one day and said I should go that evening. I was getting a bit tired of baked beans or macaroni, I must admit, but didn't wish to give trouble. That evening we went back to his house. We went round and called on several people. I think he was trying to get them to take me as a guest, but he was unsuccessful. I spent that night at his house, and also the following day. I was able to teach the little girls how to play dominoes, which game we found in the first aid haversack. We also played noughts and crosses and my little friends thought it all grand fun. Several of the [---] lady friends came in to see me. I was a bit of a curio and everyone had some friends in Australia or South Africa I should have known! Photographs were produced of Johannesburg and other towns in the Empire.

That evening, I was taken to my friend's – who had given me the shirt – house. He was a most jovial chap, laughed and talked at the top of his voice with complete disregard and filled me with confidence. Some liver sausage of some sort was given to me but I couldn't get my teeth through it, try as I would, so I had to make a joke of it and pretended to be a cat. This amused everyone and whenever I saw this man in the future, he made the actions of a cat eating a rat. The next day I was taken to a wood shed where I met an English-speaking man. He asked for particulars of myself and my Unit and gave me paper to write this down on. I was to be taken to an empty house where would I please work in the garden, to make it appear as though I was the caretaker? Of course, nothing would please me more, as I was longing for fresh air and exercise.

I stayed in this house two days and two nights, and each evening my host would bring me food for the next day, and we would go and visit friends of his, very jolly friends they were, too. I met a man who had been in America twenty years and spoke with an American accent. He took my papers, which I had filled up at some length, to the previous English-speaking chap and I had hopes that I would be away in a month. The next morning, the American turned up again with another man who, he said, had been a corporal in the Greek Army. I was to go with him. We started off out into the country and I noticed we were walking east. We walked for about 2 miles and came to a German road block. Here, we turned out into the fields and joined the road on the far side of the block. I was taken to a little tavern, or restaurant, where I met his wife and two little boys.

The tavern was situated at Hassani on the southern extremity of the main Luftwaffe base south of Athens city centre.

They made me very comfortable and gave me a little room for myself. The room was about 8 feet long and 4 wide and with the table, chair and bed, there was no room to move. I lived here, however, for three weeks, or twenty-three days to be exact. I ate the same food as the family and went out only in the evenings. It was, however, close to an aerodrome and I was able to watch the Jerry planes coming in and taking off. I also had front seats for our own raids on this airport.

A need for English books to read was getting very acute, as I had nothing whatever to do. I could not learn Greek because I had no one who could give me a start. We conversed in signs and with the help of my dialogue book. I made myself useful in sawing timber, however, which gave me much-needed exercise.

One day, a dear young lady came to see me. She spoke fairly good English and taught me a little Greek. She promised me some English books. She brought them a few days later, also some cigarettes and some underclothing she had obtained from the Red Cross. Madam was always very kind on these occasions and I was able to entertain my friends with some palm wine or coffee. The palm wine is collected, so I gather, from some palm tree, which the local inhabitants tap and [then] draw off this liquid. It is fairly potent if drunk in large quantities and had the advantage of making me sleep, in which occupation I spent much of my time. The coffee is obtained from some ground nut, which is roasted and ground like coffee and makes quite a drinkable coffee. Fosser [Fosser Parenthera], for that was the girl's Christian name, visited me on several occasions and on one, brought with her a boyfriend. This chap, Anthony by name, spoke English very well and something in his accent reminded me of C. S. [Lieutenant Costas Stathatos] who had served with my Unit to teach Greek. I asked him if by any chance he knew Costas Stathatos. He replied, "Yes, he's my brother." [...] I was now able to give him particulars of his brother, which he took back home to his sister and mother.

Anthony came to see me often and brought many books, also a letter which I would take to his brother on my return. His cousin also wrote to me, saying that a certain English man would call on me with a view to getting me back to Egypt. She herself would come, only it was too risky. I also met George who was the son of the Greek Consul in Suez. He spoke good English and brought me books to read, also I borrowed a sweater from him, without which I should have frozen to death, as it was getting very cold now.

Altogether, I spent quite a good time with these friends of mine, especially after getting the books.

Previous to the arrival of the books, I had spent my time in watching the Germans training on the hillside. Was it possible they were training to move behind sheep? I spent hours watching them move slowly up and down the hill, but they were just too far to distinguish what they were doing. It gave me great delight, however, when during an air raid on the landing ground to the [---] some plane, either by accident or intentionally, dropped a bomb right in the middle of them. They were all lying down during the raid and I do not think it would have been possible to see them unless, of course, they were all looking up, which is quite likely.

I wondered if I might get orders to go and blow up some planes on the 'drome, as we used to do at Agedabia or Sirte in North Africa. I should, of course, need explosives and it would be unwise to do them until the invasion was on its way, as the Greeks would be punished. My old and original friend, Costas, had found me. It seems I had been moved without his knowledge and he had only been able to find out where I had gone a week later. He came straight out to see me and we embraced. I was really glad to see him again, as I thought I had lost him and had never thanked him. Came the time when my host of the tavern went into the country to see his parents, and I suppose to get more provisions, for as far as I could see, their whole living depended on selling palm wine at about 3/- a litre (1,500 drachmae) and occasionally a few fried fish to customers. During the ten days that he was away, Madam would have to do the purchasing and hauling firewood with her two little boys. I merely managed to saw it up for them.

Olivey was still troubled that the British, and LRDG especially, had been defeated in the Dodecanese. With little else to occupy his thoughts, he pondered how such a thing could have happened, returning to his theory that the Wehrmacht had made cunning use of farm animals.

I realised that the Germans had trained a unit to move up quickly behind sheep, whose bells were likely to lull the enemy into a false security, then had allowed them to creep up and capture Lieutenant John Kay at Levitha and also Lieutenant Brown at Leros. It was clear to me that if they suddenly appeared over a trench and threatened the occupant with a grenade and at the same time warned them to keep quiet and come out of the trench, they could remove troops from right under our noses. It would take a very brave man to then give a warning, and in any case a grenade would silence him for ever. The snipers on the opposite hill could easily be left to keep the heads down of anyone who might attempt to look over the top.

> That was, no doubt, why my trench had been left alone, because we had continued to fire at Leros and it was therefore impossible for them to creep up close without being seen. I remembered the Greeks had asked in Leros, why do the Germans always have so many sheep with them? I remembered how a Greek had arrived at the fort at 320 with a complaint that his sheep had been shot by the Italians, but he had never come to me. Was it possible that this was a spy who came to see what our defences were like? Had his sheep really been shot by the Italians? I could remember no occasion when they had used rifles.
>
> Why had that fellow started calling us "Aussie"? If a spy had come up, he had most likely noticed we were not English troops, but would not recognise Rhodesians. Now, when I thought of it, he had come up about the time we had seen the submarine on the occasion of the air raids. Of course he was a spy. And the shouting, both at Levitha and during the battle at 320, was only to find out our positions. How cunning these Huns had been. Yes, that was clear.

It is quite possible that Olivey's men had indeed been mistaken for 'Aussies', especially if some had worn their issue slouch hat, similar to that favoured by Australians.

> But how had they trained the sheep to ring their bells only when required, as they obviously did at night? It came to me in a flash. Of course, at night the sheep would not be necessary and the men could carry the bells. The sheep would be left behind on the hilltop, having been brought to the spot required by truck.
>
> The lamb's bleat was easy for anyone practical to make as a call for assistance – the sound of movement was hidden when the ewe ran to its lamb. The noise of the mule going up or down was practised by a German toy at which they are so clever. That a mule never whinnies had been overlooked, or else they had no horse, which would usually be used. The birds' wings were some sort of rocket device from a catapult. The operator of the catapult had been unable to see me from the top of his rock, but my shoulder

> might have been obvious from the rising moon. The one bray, I remembered, had been very mechanical and was, no doubt, their success signal. After all, I had heard it in Leros village, also as coming from their Headquarters, as well as below on the road in the valley. Any troops who were captured by this squad – and I believe they were not keen on capturing men, rather in driving them with their star shells into the hands of the troops below – such prisoners would be kept separate until there was no fear of them getting away. They had not counted on anybody letting the squads pass right over them, and I began to wonder if any of my patrol experienced the same thing and if they had been wise enough to remain quiet. I should only discover this on my return to Cairo, and at the same time I ought to try and warn H.Q. of what I had found out. […]
>
> It was plain as day to me now. Of course, they would be unable to collect the sheep again at night, hence their presence on the hills when I came to move. I remembered now that these sheep had no bells, a fact I noticed at the time but thought nothing of. Hitler's circus was no circus after all, but just a conjuring trick.

Having satisfied himself that his present situation was due to an enemy that relied on trickery rather than superior military skills and tactics, Olivey was better able to accept his lot. On sunny days at the restaurant, he would relax in a deck chair and enjoy the books his Greek friends had provided. Sometimes, an otherwise monotonous routine would be interrupted by an unexpected visitor.

> Certainly, these Greeks were very kind to me, always bringing some present or other in the way of cigarettes, vest or pants, and I was always overjoyed at seeing them. I hope certainly to look them up again.
>
> One Sunday, my old friend Costas turned up again and told me to be ready to move on Tuesday evening. I was unable to discover where I was to go to, but he had obviously been busy, and as it was a month since I had given my particulars, I thought perhaps now, at last, I was to move to Cairo. Tuesday came and my host had still

not returned and Costas had arrived at about 3 p.m. I was to leave at 5 p.m. Fortunately, just about 4 p.m. Costas [the tavern owner] arrived home. The position was explained to him. He seemed rather doubtful and seemed to think this was a grave risk in taking me away. How kind he was, obviously still willing that I should live at his expense and the risk it all entailed to him. I wrote a short note to all my English-speaking friends and told them I hoped to meet them all again, thanking them for all their kindness. Leaving my home address with my host and with many fond farewells, Costas and I set off back along the road I had come. We left with the little son, who came with us through the German road block. We walked boldly past the sentry on the road, who was busy with a lorry, and as we passed, the young son then turned back and we proceeded. I was first taken to an underground cellar which held a number of people who appeared to be purchasing flour and was, I presume, a front of the black market. I think Costas had slipped up in bringing me here, as I was quickly taken out again and walked up and down side streets until I had quite lost my way. I then found myself on the road from which I had made my escape and here, I met my friend of the chewing cats meat who was delighted to see me.

Olivey was escorted to a park and there said goodbye to his two friends. He would not see them again. He was joined now by another man, known as Fotakis, who was strolling arm in arm with a young woman, Liberty, and together they walked back the way Olivey had come.

I whispered, "Do you speak English?" He replied, "Yes, I do, but don't speak now" (as with all these changes I wanted to know where I was going to). We obtained a taxi and we drove for some little way. I was by now certain we were going to a boat.

When we pulled up, the girl, Liberty, went off and we took a walk up a side road. My English-speaking friend now informed me that this was an organisation to help escaping prisoners. Liberty returned and we proceeded to her brother's house. There, in a room, I explained myself and how I came to be in Athens. I produced what little evidence I could to show I was a British officer. Unfortunately, I had very little to prove this. These people were obviously worried lest I should be a Gestapo agent, which, I suppose, was natural in a country where this plague abounds. We talked for some time and I was, at last, more or less accepted. I met Liberty's brother and his wife and their mother. We played poker, and as I had no money, it was rather a one-sided game. I managed to win from the start, however, and soon had won 15,000 D., worth about 3d I discovered afterwards, but at the time I thought it great wealth. We had a very good meal of spaghetti, potatoes, cheese, butter and bread. Liberty, who spoke English very well, apologised for the supper as they had not been expecting me. Little did they know, it was the first square meal I had had for a month. After dinner, four liqueurs were produced. I politely sipped mine, which was very good, and Liberty had one. As no one else would have one, Liberty and I finished them all over a game of rummy. She was a charming girl, Liberty, with a grand sense of humour and seemed to be laughing all the time. I learnt that it was her Saint Day the next day and so she was not going to the office. In Greece, the young people celebrate their Saint Day and not their birthday and a party is usually given.

I was surprised at the abundance of cakes that Liberty had. The high cost of living was certainly no object with this family. Afterwards, I learnt that to have money these days in Greece, it was necessary to work for the Germans and Liberty's brother was something in a [---] works, which accounted for it. Liberty had a grand party and a whole crowd of people turned up for it. I had to stay in the bedroom but Liberty would bring some plates full of cakes and sweets. I gave her a birthday kiss, which I much enjoyed. I called her my sister, which seemed to please her. That evening I was taken away from this house. These people had been so kind to me. I never saw the mother to thank her, but I shall call again someday. Liberty gave me some cakes to take with me and promised to find the home I was staying in and she would then come and see me. I on my part promised to take her out to dinner and dance when the Germans were driven out of Greece and if I was back here. We went in a taxi back into Athens and here I met Fotakis again. He took me up some stairs which led to a dentist's establishment. I gathered I should spend the night here in a little room. I now learnt that the water in Athens was turned off at 10 in the morning and that electricity was rationed. Some eggs, bread and cheese were brought for me and I was left for the night in the flat. Next morning, I spent the first few hours in watching the crowd in the street through the shutters. A number of Italians in uniforms mixed with the crowd and I learned later that when Italy had thrown in her hand, the Italians had behaved very badly and betrayed the Greeks to the Germans. I was told that the first thing the Italians had tried to do was to sell their arms. These the Greeks bought as far as possible. They had then tried to flee to [---], but the Germans had stopped most of them and it was a common sight to see two or three hundred Italians rounded up by two German soldiers. A number of Italians had said they were [---] and were now employed by the Germans in sitting on the back of food lorries and the like. Surely, this is a great nation of turncoats. The dentist arrived about 9 o'clock and with his sister I helped dust the flat until patients started to arrive. I then had to go back to my little room. I was allowed out at intervals when there was no one present. A dentist's life was not an easy one at this time, as no one had money to spend on their teeth and it was impossible to get fees paid. I felt sorry for this man who, from his photographs, had lost a lot of weight and looked old for his 30 years. We conversed in French and could not say very much, as my knowledge of French is not very extensive. That evening, Fotakis turned up again and I was again taken by taxis. This time we arrived at a house where lived Mad. [---], her husband, and little boy. The husband was out when I arrived, but he was expected back at 7 p.m. I had an opportunity to study Mad. in the meantime. We conversed in French, as she could speak no English and I could speak no Greek. Two studio photographs on the wall bore witness to the fact that she had once been fat and 40. Now – and I was given to understand, owing to the shortage of food – she had lost her fat and the stretched skin had retracted into wrinkles. She still might, however, be considered as plump on present day standards. When she spoke Greek she talked at an enormous rate which made her conversations sound rather like a Bren gun firing in bursts. Both Greek and French were punctuated with many tears, which seemed to be under wonderful control, as she could produce them at any stage of the conversation at a moment's notice, and, just as quickly, make them disappear. I gathered that life had been a hard struggle and she had had to sell all her jewels to provide food. I noticed that there was a tremendous amount of furniture in this small flat. We waited, talking in French until 9 p.m., when the husband turned up and the reason for his delay was at once obvious, as he reeked of liquor. He spoke good English, however, having had an Irish nanny. He was a sallow youth, very much younger than Mad., very dark, and looked as though he had missed his shave two days previously. He had had some business or other which the Italians, and now the Germans, had taken at a nominal figure. He was now unemployed and I should say not over anxious to be employed at anything which meant hard work. If he did do any work, it consisted of selling Mad.'s furniture and vases behind her back. His family had obviously been among the better-class people of Athens. His mother lived next door, spoke excellent English and was a charming lady. His father spoke Greek and French. I was given a little room in which I stayed for four or five days. This little room was a portion of the kitchen partitioned off. Every sound could be heard through the flat and as if this were not enough, every time the loving couple indulged in husband and wifely amusements, they would make a point of opening the door of their bedroom. As I did not really enjoy listening to the amorous noises, I would slam the door as if by the wind, but it would always be religiously opened again. I cannot for the life of me think why.

I was badly feeling the need for exercise and the need for books. How slowly the time passes when one has nothing to do and has no books. I learnt that we were to move house as this one was considered too dangerous owing to one of the occupants being pro-German. There was some difficulty in finding a house which had to be rent paid in advance for a year. I gathered that the organisation which was looking after me was going to pay this rent. I thought this rather unnecessary as I was still convinced that I should be back in Cairo for Christmas and it was now about the 14th December. We moved down to this house one evening. Mad. and I walked, taking with us a counterpane, blanket and a pillow case of the more valuable things in the house. The husband was, I now learnt, the lover, as Mad.'s husband was overseas somewhere, Mad. having been visiting Greece when war broke out. His name shall be N. [Nikolaos]. Nikolaos was not accompanying us that night as there was the house to be looked after and he would follow with the furniture next day. We walked through the Greek streets carrying our load, or rather, I carried both loads as Mad. did nothing but complain that the house we were to go to was no good. She shuffled along in her heelless shoes nearly driving me mad.

When we arrived at the house, I found it was almost a cellar, being 2 feet below the street surface. Very damp and cold, it contained a hall, a bedroom, a dining room, kitchen and bathroom and for this they had paid 35,000,000 D. for the year's rent. I had seen several gold sovereigns changing hands. The gold sovereign at this time was worth about 2,500,000 D., but to my own way of thinking, the D. was valueless, as the Germans had brought a printing press and just turned out the notes as they required to pay anyone. Any gold that fell into German hands was, of course, taken to Germany, together with any foodstuffs they might require. The black market had come into being when Greeks were starving and dying in the streets for want of food and now the price of rents and food went up almost hourly. A box of matches cost 5,000 D., an egg 15,000 D., cigarettes 1,000 D. each, so that I calculated that 5,000 D. is equal to 1d., though I doubt very much if it would have been possible to change an English £1 note and no one would look at a Palestine £1 note. The English pound note was at the time worth 19/6 in Palestine or Egypt.

D. (drachma) was the standard Greek currency; 1d was the (pre-decimal) English penny, of which there were 240 to £1.00 (one pound); 19/6, or 19 shillings and sixpence was sixpence short of £1.00.

There was a bath, no stove or anything to cook on, stone tiles on the floors and one bed. Mad. wept and groaned at the same time, and for my own part, I wondered how all the furniture would get in such a small house. I was still wandering about between dining room and kitchen when I noticed Mad. had got into, or rather, on the bed and covered herself with the quilt blanket. I wondered what I was supposed to do. Mad. made it immediately obvious that I was to share the bed with her. There seemed nothing else for it, as I certainly didn't fancy a night on the bare stones, and except for the bath, there was nothing else even to sit on. Mad., wise woman, had kept on her underclothes. I, playing the perfect gent, kept my trousers on. Even so, I spent a restless night and was glad when morning came. The furniture arrived at about 11 o'clock and the little cellar was at once full of stuff, leaving an alley way of about 3 feet wide, which trickled from front door to kitchen and bathroom, with a branch line to the window in the bedroom. Still all the furniture had not arrived and Mad., again in tears, groaning and talking at a tremendous rate, went back to see about the remainder of the furniture. I was given a settee in the hall. The settee had more than half the springs broken but I spent many hours there, day and night, and it served its purpose. I can safely say these were my most uncomfortable days in my army career, and this included two years in the desert in blazing sun or cold winter. To start with, there was no food. The first three days, all I had to eat was a plate of peas and an [---] of apples. Fotakis had got lost in the move, and as he didn't know where the house was and his house was a secret, I couldn't see how we should ever contact him again. I wrote a note to Anthony and asked Nikolaos to take it to him as I hoped he might rescue me. And I had decided to return to my tavern if nothing turned up over Christmas. Nikolaos seldom slept in the house as his father

> was terrified that he would be caught with an English officer in his house. Mad. was always grousing and I was glad when she would go out to try and find Fotakis. I had a good idea that, while out, she would have a good meal also. It is wonderful what the human frame can stand, however, and so for four days I had only water, nothing to read, nowhere to walk and only my thoughts to amuse myself with.

Olivey's situation was far from ideal, but still preferable to life as a prisoner of war, even though, as a captain, Olivey would have enjoyed certain privileges in an *Offizierlager*, or officers' camp. The ORs had to make do in an ordinary *Stammlager*. South African Philip Hayter was in the Natal Carbineers when he was captured near Tobruk in 1942. He was at Moosburg, a camp near Munich, when the LRDG arrived there from Leros.

'I was detailed to go down to the railway station under guard and get these blokes out of the trucks. When they arrived, we opened the trucks and this was a crowd of Rhodesians. They had been in the train for twenty-one days, since leaving Athens. They were the Long Range Desert Group (LRDG) who had been caught on the island of Kos [sic] in the Mediterranean, one of the Greek Islands and they talked about their officer called John Olivey who had eventually escaped in Athens. Whilst they were marching through Athens to the station he had escaped and I made friends with his driver, a fellow called Jenkinson. These fellows were in a dreadful state. You have never seen anything like it. When we lifted them up, the lice were just falling out of their sleeves and out of their collars, they had hardly had any food for three weeks and they could not walk. We took them to the wash house and took off their clothes and they were put into a steriliser and were deloused. We helped them wash and shave and get themselves into reasonable shape. We made hot drinks for them out of our [Red Cross] parcels and walked them around. I became friendly with these blokes and we had Christmas with them, they were a nice crowd, particularly old Jenkie; he was a great friend of mine.'

After he was repatriated, Phil Hayter moved to Rhodesia, where he would meet John Olivey and eventually marry his daughter, Annabel. But in December 1943, the war was far from over and those in captivity faced an uncertain future, as did Hayter's future father-in-law, whose dream of returning home was fading with each passing day.

> Right up to Christmas Eve, I had faith that I should be in Cairo for Christmas. I felt certain that my faith would not desert me. On Christmas Eve, I felt most depressed and felt there was now nothing to believe in. I had counted so much on getting back to Cairo for Christmas. Now I began to wonder what was the meaning of all this greed and avarice in the world.
>
> On Christmas Eve, Fotakis turned up full of apologies, as surely he should have been. He had been found wandering somewhere near looking up at the windows. He knew the area, but not the house. From now on, things were better. It seemed that money he had given Mad. and Nikolaos for food for me had been spent on transport of furniture. He now decided to buy my food himself, and it being Christmas Eve, brought some meat for stew, some potatoes, white bread and butter. I must say that when he did buy food it was good, but from now on, Mad. took no interest in what I had to eat, having all her meals outside the house. She would leave the house at about 9 a.m. and often not return until evening. I was left to cook my food as best I could. It is not surprising, under the circumstances, if she found a chair or two missing, as I had to have fire wood after all. I must say I loathed this couple and spared no pains in showing Nikolaos exactly what I thought of him leaving me night after night with his mistress. I had also discovered that Mad. had been Fotakis's former mistress, so that he was, no doubt, trying to do her a good turn at my expense.
>
> I had by this time rebelled against being kept in the house all day and night and used to take a walk for an hour down the back streets of the area. There seemed to me very little danger of anyone stopping me. I was, therefore, able to get a little exercise. I missed the sun though, and quite longed to be able to heat up

> my body in the sun again. I had asked Fotakis to remove me from this house, as I felt I could no longer stick the life I was living and that I would rather make a break for it on my own. I felt certain I could have got back to Cairo had I not fallen into the hands of this organisation. [...]

Olivey was especially concerned that his wife might by this time have received notification that he was missing, presumed killed, and more than anything wanted to let her know otherwise. As the situation continued, he became increasingly despondent with the lackadaisical attitude and general unreliability of those around him, while at the same time, despairing of the cold, miserable, living conditions.

> One day Fotakis came and told me I must be ready to move at 5 p.m. the next day, that I should meet him at the corner in the street, that he had found me a nice house to live in where I should be well looked after. This I did and met him at the corner, only to be told that it wasn't possible that night. I then returned with the promise that the next night would be the time. The next night, the same thing happened and so for three or four nights, until one night we went to meet a Greek officer who would take me to the house. The Greek officer did not turn up, so again, it was off.
>
> Two days later Fotakis called at the house and told me I was to bring my things, that he had found a house for me where I should be very comfortable. Mad. had gone out at 9 a.m. that morning and had not returned yet and it was now 5.30 p.m. M's [sic] mother had called earlier in the afternoon, however.
>
> To answer the door of this house, I used to examine who was at the door through the shutters of the window and if it was someone I did not know, I would, of course, not open the door and they would eventually go away. I had only been caught once, and, that time, Nikolaos had just gone out, and hearing a knock, thought he had returned, having forgotten something. On opening the door, I found a man and his notebook saying something in Greek. I replied, Ochi! Ochi! No! No! What he wanted, I did not know, and if he was the man to examine the electric meter, he must have

been most surprised at my actions. The milkman often came, as he was hoping to supply Mad. with milk and butter in exchange for her womanly services, thinking Mad. was living alone! I now left without a word and should have loved to hear Mad. on her return. Her grouses had almost driven me mad, but I should have loved to hear this last grouse. I must say I feel I owe this family nothing and hope never to see them again. Nikolaos had turned out [to be] a waster of the worst kind of cad, and Mad. a greedy avarist who thought only of herself and what she could make out of anyone. It was impossible to feel sorry for such people, even if they were near [to] starvation themselves.

Fotakis and I met an A. and two Greek officers up the road and I was handed over to the Greek 2nd Lieutenant E. [Elias Georgopoulos], who took me off to his house.

I met here his uncle who had spent fourteen years in America as a grocer before 1914, an M. B. and his wife who had not been to America and spoke no English, and their son C., who spoke quite good English. I was given a little room with a comfortable bed and a desk and my meals were brought to me in this room. I had hoped that my room would have a southerly aspect so I might get the sun, but it had an east view on to some high houses opposite and so I was to get no sun. The only place I could walk was either round and round the dining room table when there was no one else in the house, or up on the roof top at night when the neighbours could not see me. My craving for the sun was very great. Few people know how much they enjoy the sun until they are kept from it, and now I had not been in the sun for over a month. These good people made me very welcome and I looked forward to enjoying my stay with them. It was wonderful to get nicely cooked and regular meals, also cheerful people to live with. Nevertheless, I felt the need for books. It is strange how difficult it seemed to get my English books, though I knew people would be only too pleased to lend me books. My contacts all seemed frightened to go and ask. What a strange country this is where everyone is frightened of his friends, where everyone fears that even their best friend will sell them to the Germans for money. Having no books and now living

> in comfort, I started to think of the troubles of this world of ours, of capitalism, communism and religion.

Olivey was of the opinion that in Greece the minority who favoured communism were 'merely a gang of malcontent have-nots' who envied those even slightly better off than themselves. On the other hand, Olivey considered the average Greek a poor capitalist, who often excelled in business when starting from scratch, but seemed content to generate only enough cash to live comfortably, with little interest in investing further.

> This has been proved again and again in the Dominions, Colonies and U.S.A. The Greek, having built up a sizeable trading store from nothing, would then sell out and with sufficient capital to last the remainder of his life, he will [...] return to Greece. I feel that the Greeks as a race are very avaristic, and, in my own case, I am convinced that I was being kept as a good paying concern. The generous British Army were quite prepared to pay for the return of their soldiers and pay very handsomely for the return of their officers, but obviously, it paid someone to delay these returns as long as possible, [by] inventing all sorts of excuses why it was impossible for me to return. At one time I was told they were waiting for orders from Headquarters, at another that they were not certain if I was an Englishman, yet again that there were difficulties, but that they were organising my journey down to the coast (10 miles at the most!). I could see no possible way of getting away from this trap, having fallen into the clutches of these men.

Unsurprisingly, those who fought in the Second World War often contemplated what life might be like afterwards, and in this, Olivey was no exception. He imagined a world with 'the banks, then the land, then the mines, the shops, the ships and all industries and amusements' nationalised. Schools would be 'available to everyone', and, together with hospitals, would be free. Those prepared to work would deserve to be rewarded, while those who shirked their responsibilities could expect fewer 'comforts' and 'luxuries'.

Capitalism would be dispensed with and replaced with a new world order, a United States of Europe and a new form of government: Idealism.

> And so I thought, during those long hours of waiting, with nothing to read. Continually waiting for I knew not what, but something to happen, perhaps for orders for me to move back to Cairo on some secret ship or aircraft. Perhaps the promised invasion would soon take place. A number of houses in Greece have secret wireless sets and on these it was possible to get the news from London. All legalised sets were sealed in such a way as to make it possible to pick up the local station only. C. used to listen to [the BBC?] most nights at their Greek transmission of 9 p.m. local time and would pass the news to me. One night the King of Greece spoke, sympathising with the people of Greece on the bombing of Piraeus, the harbour for Athens. He said it was necessary, in view of the coming liberation, which was close at hand. The American and British air forces had bombed Piraeus and the electric station, causing great damage. In one slit trench near the electric station, the German soldiers had ordered the civilian population out of the trench so that they might occupy it. Imagine the joy of the Greek people when a bomb falls right in this trench, killing the German soldiers. Surely this was an act of God.
>
> It was surely the act of God which picked out most of the houses that contained Germans on this occasion, for although the Greeks had suffered heavy casualties, the Germans had suffered far higher in proportion.

The next paragraph in Olivey's memoir addresses his wife directly.

> I had now borrowed some English books so that I was able to spend my time in reading and writing this letter to you. The hours now passed by very much more rapidly and I hope I was in better temper to those kind people who were looking after my interests. We do not realise the debt we owe to books until we have to go without them. I was also able to give a little assistance to C. and

> P. who were both learning English. We had great discussions on forms of government and I found that these people believed that England would take over the Government of Greece. I supposed that this was never our policy even in our own Dominions and it was most unlikely that we should try the [---] the government of another state, except as far as its foreign policy was concerned.

John Olivey stopped writing at this point. The story does not end here, however.

CHAPTER 14

The Cicero Connection

John Olivey's movements in the first quarter of 1944 can be told thanks to operation reports and the narrative of an interview provided to Defence Headquarters in Salisbury, Rhodesia, in or about July 1944. Olivey spent more than four months in hiding, moving from one safe house to another. He later recalled:

'I stayed within doors by day, but ventured abroad at dusk. If ever I was accosted by a policeman, I had only to mutter "Gestapo", upon which he would immediately retire.'

At last, Olivey was presented with an opportunity to return to the Middle East.

'I fell in with an officer of the Greek Army [Elias Georgopoulos] who was himself most anxious to get to Egypt. I told him that, if he would make the arrangements for me to go, I would take him with me and would pay his fare. An evening or two later he reported that the arrangements had been made. …

'The skipper of a small Greek ship had been ordered by the Germans to carry a considerable cargo of sugar and oil to their garrison on the island of Chios, which lies off the Turkish coast. As soon as his mission was known, he was surreptitiously approached by a number of Greeks who offered to pay him handsomely if he would carry them to Turkey, instead. After all, it was easy enough; for his ship would be given safe conduct by the Germans across the Aegean Sea. But, once he had made the voyage, he could hardly return; so that, to put it plainly, it had to be made worth his while to undertake the venture. It was made worth his while, and he promised to do the job. It was as two of this human cargo that the Greek officer and I were to sail.

'One night, towards the end of March, 1944, he and I entered a taxi in one of Athens' streets. We drove to the outskirts of the city. There we left the taxi, because we were approaching the "control" [checkpoint]. This was strict, with a post upon every road. The taxi proceeded without us, while we were guided through the backyards of private premises, until we were beyond the "control". There the taxi was waiting to pick us up. After several miles we left the taxi for a bus, and early the following morning we reached the coast.

'The spot was desolate. There was, of course, no harbour; and when the ship arrived, it would have to lie off. When it would arrive, we did not know. All we could do was to wait and to hope for the best.'

Olivey had reached Porto Rafti, south-east of Athens. There was no alternative now but to live rough in the countryside, sleeping in the hills or in caves.

'As I have said before, we were but two of the intending passengers. Of these there were no less than one hundred and five; and, as the days went by, but no ship appeared, I could hardly believe that so great a number of prospective refugees could hope to escape detection. We were all supposed to be in hiding; but nobody hid. Had any one of us been accosted, he had no answer to give – much less any explanation of the company he kept. But everyone accepted most casually our perilous plight and seemed to see no reason for caution, or even for care. In desperation, I would often enough withdraw and walk or sit by myself, apart from the crowd: but, so sure as I did this, my absence would be remarked, and others would come running to join me and show their goodwill.

'For two full weeks this state of affairs prevailed, and why we were never discovered I cannot tell. And then, at last, the ship came.

'It was only a caique and was heavily laden with the cargo which the Germans had put aboard. But this, with the skipper's consent, we soon threw into the sea and so made room for a number of passengers. Even so, only seventy-five could be taken aboard, and thirty had to be left.

'Remembering that many of these thirty had paid as much as fifty pounds in gold apiece for their passage, but I had paid only five, I was very much touched by their insistence that I must take precedence in any case.

'Concealed beneath tarpaulins, we sailed that night. More than one German patrol boat came alongside: but the skipper fobbed them off somehow, and nobody came aboard. We made the island of Tinos just about dawn: there we lay up for the day and sailed for Chios that night. When we were nearing Chios, we changed our course, to enter Turkish waters after a very short time.

'We proposed to land south of Çeşme; but this the Turks would not have; so the skipper beached the caique a little way down the coast. Only one soul of us all failed to reach shore.

'With others, I walked to Çeşme and saw the Greek Consul there. A week later, the Greek officer and I were taken to the British Consulate at Izmir, where I was made very welcome. A few days later I left for Cyprus. There I was issued with uniform, and thence I was flown to Cairo.

'My escape had been made.'

Even then, Olivey's adventure was not yet at an end. It was now April 1944. After reaching Izmir, he reported to Major Alexander Caridia of Military Intelligence section 9 (MI9), responsible for escape and evasion and the return of British and other prisoners of war. Before long, he was approached by Security Intelligence Middle East (SIME) and asked if he would escort a young German woman to Cairo.

According to one source, 'When the British representative took one look at Nele [sic] he said, "That girl is a German. I'll have nothing to do with her. The only good Germans are dead Germans."' One can perhaps guess the identity of the 'British representative'.

'Nielia', or Cornelia, Kapp was the daughter of the German Consul-General in Sofia, Bulgaria. After having come to Ankara, Turkey, to escape the Allied air raids in Sofia, she became secretary to SS-Sturmbannführer Ludwig Moyzisch, whose official role was assistant commercial attaché at the German Embassy in Ankara. He was also Ankara's chief Security Service (SD) officer, answerable to the Reich Security Main Office (RSHA).

Kapp's job was to translate English and French press articles into German. In April 1944, she defected to the Allies and disclosed that a spy known as Cicero (Turkish: Çiçero) was in the employ of Moyzisch. Initially, at least, Kapp seems to have been considered as unreliable by British Intelligence. Drawing on a report dated 9 May 1944, MI5 was of the opinion that '[Moyzisch] did not really know her and realised that she was slightly "mental" so did not give her any confidential work. Therefore she cannot divulge any information of value and MOYZISCH himself was not responsible for her particularly as she was mentally deficient.'

In fact, Cicero was the code name for Elyesa Bazna, valet to the British ambassador in Ankara, Sir Hughe Knatchbull-Hugessen, and he was indeed providing Moyzisch with British secret information.

Olivey later told 'Brick' Broderick of his involvement with Kapp:

'We travelled by Greek caique down the Aegean stopping at night in shore, flying the Turkish flag past Rhodes in the early morning to Cyprus (with the Greek flag) the trip took about a week.

'We were both in civvies, she was supposed to be my wife, and I the owner. I was armed with a revolver by M.I.9 and told to shoot her if the Jerries caught up with us. (We had a very pleasant trip, except that the caique had hit a sand bank and the prop bent made the stern bump in the water!!). She had to keep out of sight by day, and she and I kept watch for the crew of 2 or 3 at night!'

In Cyprus, Olivey and Kapp were met by an officer of 'A' Force, specialists in deception, and another, more senior, figure, believed to have been Colonel (acting Brigadier) Raymund J. Maunsell, head of SIME. Olivey learned that they were to continue their journey incognito, he in the uniform of a private soldier, and Kapp disguised as a member of the South African Women's Auxiliary Service. So attired, they proceeded by air to Haifa and on to Cairo, arriving on 25 April 1944. Olivey recalled:

'Her story to me was that she had offered herself to the Yanks, who had no way of taking her out. (The Jerries were watching the airport and station.) The Yanks handed her over to the British, Sir Hugh Knatchbull-Hugessen gave me the once over at a sundowner party in Ankara and I was told to hand her over to the O.C. M.I.9 Cairo.'

In a letter to 'Stuka' Stokes, Olivey commented of his involvement with Military Intelligence and Cornelia Kapp, 'it finishes off the Greek story very well', as indeed it did.

At the end of July 1944, Olivey returned from home leave to join what was now A (Rhodesian) Squadron, reassuming his preferred role, this time as OC Z1 Patrol. Following a brief operation in Albania, he deployed to Greece in September. Towards year's end, he found himself involved in an internal conflict between a people who, months before, he had trusted with his life. Now, British forces were tasked with supporting the Greek government in its efforts against the Communist-led Greek People's Liberation Army (ELAS). On 11 December, Olivey's jeep came under fire in the area of Omonia Square in Athens city centre. He and his driver, Rifleman Arthur S. Botha, were wounded, the latter fatally. Olivey was thus very nearly killed by a people who, shortly before, had risked their lives to help him. Recently decorated for his conduct on Leros, he was recommended by Lieutenant Colonel Lloyd Owen for a third MC:

'Captain OLIVEY was commanding a patrol of L.R.D.G., which was landed with Jeeps on the west coast of the PELEPONNESE in September 1944. His patrol was used under POMPFORCE to follow up and destroy the enemy through Greece. Soon after landing he was in action near CORINTH and then crossed the canal and was among the first troops to enter ATHENS. His patrol, mounting .5 MG's on their Jeeps, then pursued the enemy as far as FLORINA and Captain OLIVEY showed very great courage and determination throughout this pursuit. His patrol then returned to ATHENS where they remained until the fighting, which began in the city, when Captain OLIVEY'S patrol were used in efforts to clear the streets of snipers. In one such action Captain OLIVEY himself firing a M.G. from his Jeep drove down a street in ATHENS and cleared the enemy from a strong point inflicting casualties and taking prisoners. On another occasion he was patrolling a street in a Jeep when he was fired on by snipers and his driver was severely wounded. The Jeep was damaged from short range fire and in a gallant attempt to rescue his driver Captain OLIVEY was himself wounded in the head and arm. However he managed to drag the driver away from the vehicle but not before he was shot dead by further sniping. Captain OLIVEY then succeeded in himself escaping and obtaining the assistance of an armoured vehicle. Throughout these operations Captain OLIVEY shewed complete disregard for his own safety under fire and a cheerfulness in danger which was a magnificent example to the men under his command.'

It is not known if the recommendation was even submitted. But, for whatever reason, the award was never made.

By March 1945 Olivey had recovered and was back with Z1 Patrol, this time in Istria. There, cooperation between Tito's communist Partisans and their allies was fragile at the best of times, and there were frequent misunderstandings and disagreements. On 6 May 1945, just two days before the end of the war in Europe, Olivey and his men were detained, and not for the first time. They were freed a day later. As Captain C. Stuart Manning, drawing on the War Diary of the LRDG, recounted in his unpublished history of the Rhodesian Squadron (post-desert phase), 'the patrol was taken before the local Commander who released them with many apologies and much wine. Olivey had lived up to his reputation of being in trouble when the whole show was over!'

Olivey might have finished the war as a major, at least, but he had been less interested in promotion than he was in continuing to lead from the front. Seniority brought a different level of responsibility, with less likelihood of seeing action. In his book about the LRDG, *Providence their Guide*, David Lloyd Owen would appraise Olivey thus:

'For nearly three years in the desert he had commanded a Patrol. He was a good leader, and quite fearless. His had often been the task of transporting David Stirling and his Special Air Service parties on their forays into enemy-occupied airfields.

'Then when we left the desert, and went to reorganise at the Cedars in Lebanon, John Olivey became second-in-command in the Squadron which I was then commanding. This meant irksome administration, and juggling with the whole tiresome range of military proformas. John disliked this kind of soldiering, and the forms suffered in his rather haphazard care. Very soon he was back in charge of a Patrol, which was the life he loved and understood.'

Having achieved his 'boyish hopes and aims', Captain Olivey MC and Bar returned to Rhodesia, and he and Mickey were demobilised to begin life together at Sawerombi. He would father five more children: Peter, twins Rosalind and Dierdre, and twins Anthony and Charles (the latter was killed in 1978 during the Rhodesian Bush War).

He was instrumental in building the Anglican church of St George's in the Mountains at Melsetter; the foundation stone was laid on 23 April 1954 and the church was consecrated in October 1956. Olivey was admitted as a lay reader and often conducted Sunday church services.

John Richard Olivey, farmer, war hero, 'Lay Vicar' of Melsetter, died suddenly at his home at Sawerombi, Rhodesia, on 9 July 1968. He was 62.

APPENDIX I

Missing in Action

The following is from John Olivey's Operation Report No. 107, compiled just one day after his return from Levitha.

'2230 hrs. M.L. arrived in RV. Bay and was contacted, also three other ranks who had been in hiding further in the bay put off in an assault boat and boarded the M.L., (1. of these was the W/T OP and 1. Rgt Sigs and one who had been guarding the P.O.W.)

'At this time also a light was seen and a boat returned to the cove where the medical officer, with his orderly and the wounded man were found. These were also taken aboard the M.L.'

These extracts are interesting on two points: the apparently erroneous number of evacuees – eight, including Olivey and Rupping, rather than the seven mentioned in most contemporary accounts – and, significantly, the retrieval from their hiding place of two of the six assault boats.

One would expect that the escapees' boats were brought back to Leros with the motor launch. Indeed, the after-action report of Leutnant Dietzsch (11./Lw.-Jg.Rgt.21) states that just four assault boats were recovered.

Dietzsch also records: 'Enemy losses: 3 dead, 2 officers and 35 men captured (including 4 men who were brought in on 29.10.43 by a reconnaissance party)'.

The same number of fatalities is corroborated by Ron Hill: 'One of the two NZs who had been wounded in the face died the next morning and was buried by the Germans with [a] guard of honour.

One other NZ was wounded in the foot and two others killed but by the time we were evacuated their bodies had not been recovered.'

And yet, four men, not three, were lost on Levitha. Hill also recalled:

'At about 3 p.m. Captain Sutherland sent off a patrol of two men, accompanied by one German POW, to bring water from the boats for the prisoners and to recce the situation from that point. This patrol did not return and it is believed was ambushed and killed. Neither man was brought in [as a] POW whilst we were on the island.'

After his release from German captivity, Corporal J. E. (Jim) Gill told the Davison family what he knew about missing Troopers Douglas Davison and John Bowler. Doug's father passed on the details in a letter to his son, Bill, who was serving overseas:

'To summarise, – Six of them were holding a position on the extreme right of a long low range of hills country covered with huge boulders and bush, cut up with deep narrow gorges. Gill's party about a mile from main crowd (Lt Sutherlands) Having not heard from Sutherland for 8 or 9 hrs and they could see that they were going to be cut off Doug set off to find out whether they should stay to the east [or coast?] or get out while they could Gill watched him from where he was getting along alright almost to objective was sure then that he had got there as he could see Sutherlands position from where he was Gill and party hid up for 4 days before giving themselves up but on meeting the others a week later found out Doug was not accounted for Germans told Gill that they had found Johnnie Bowler dead and gave Gill pay book. Germans were all over the island but did not say anything about Doug's body. Gill thinks he must have been killed near Sutherland's camp. – Cemetery with five of the boys' grave [sic] when Gill was there – Thinks Germans may have found Doug's body & buried since and information not been sent out.'

Gill had marked on a sketch map the location of the island's little cemetery, next to a chapel by the home of the Kambosos family, then, as now, the island's only residents. Gill had also indicated where John Bowler was killed – just inland from the landing place of Section 2.

As stated by Ron Hill, one New Zealander died of his wounds on 25 October. This was evidently Hector Mallett, whose mortal remains, together with those of Herbert Federmann, are accounted for. (Another New Zealander, Trooper Archibald Penhall, died in hospital on the mainland.) It is reasonable to assume that Mallett, Federmann, and, presumably, John Bowler were buried at or close to the chapel cemetery on Levitha, together with the two Italians who had lost their lives when 'Brandenburg' paratroopers seized the island on 18 October. This would account for the five burials mentioned by Gill. (According to Dietzsch, no Germans lost their lives, the only casualties being two men wounded.)

Available records show that Mallett and Federmann were later exhumed from Levitha for reburial at Kos and in 1957 reinterred at Rhodes. Inexplicably, there is no mention of field graves for either John Bowler or Douglas Davison.

With the nearest landfall an uninhabited islet nearly 2 miles from Levitha, and with all assault boats accounted for, it is safe to assume that other than the seven evacuated during the night of 24/25 October, no one else made it off the island, except as a prisoner of war.

Why, then, do available records mention only two field burials? If Ron Hill is correct in that the two 'missing' men had with them a German prisoner, the possibility exists that the trio might have been engaged by either side as a result of being misidentified. In the circumstances, only one body (Bowler) may have been found and provided with a proper burial.

Was Davison killed without anybody realising? A characteristic of Levitha is its many low-lying clumps of phrygana and maquis – thick vegetation that can provide ideal cover in an otherwise barren landscape. As Olivey observed, German troops would throw hand grenades or fire into likely hiding places. Someone killed while in concealment may not be found until later, and for practical reasons then provided with a simple field burial.

There is another possibility. The area where Section 2 operated is bordered on the southern seaward side by a cliff that varies in height and gradient. If someone were to perish there, they might never be discovered.

Unless or until the mystery is solved, both Davison and Bowler will continue to be officially listed as missing, commemorated at the Athens Memorial, along with the names of others with no known grave.

Appendix II

Levitha: 'Olforce'

Section 1

Arger, Lance Corporal Arthur – POW
Brodrick, Trooper Sidney – POW
Deegan, Private Matthew – POW
Federmann, Gunner Herbert – Killed on 24 October 1943
Fraser, Private William 'Jock' – POW
Gunn, Private David 'Boozie' – POW
Harris, Lance Corporal J. E. (Jack) – POW
Kay, Lieutenant John H. – POW
Kevan, Trooper John D. 'Flossie' – POW
Lyle, Private Douglas F. 'Titch' – POW
Maidwell, Rifleman Frank – POW
MacKay, Private John 'Daisy' – POW
Patch, Gunner J. D. (Jim) – POW
Riley, Signalman Denis – POW
Van Heerden, Rifleman Louis J. 'Vic' – POW*
Vogel, Gunner P. J. – POW
Warrington, Trooper R. W. G. – POW

---

* In what was largely a German propaganda exercise, a recruiting drive was conducted among prisoners of war who were encouraged to join the German forces as members of the British Free Corps. An attempt was made to recruit Vic van Heerden, who later submitted a report detailing what he knew of renegade prisoners.

Evacuated to Leros

Bradfield, Lance Corporal Thomas L.
Lawson, Captain Richard P.
Murphy, Lance Corporal Vincent J. 'Spud'
Olivey, Captain John R.
Rupping, Gunner Jacobus F. 'Jack'
Unidentified Rhodesian
Unidentified signaller

Section 2

Bowler, Trooper John T. – Missing, presumed killed
Burgess, Lance Corporal Walter H. – POW
Davison, Trooper Douglas A. – Missing, presumed killed
Dobson, Sergeant Edwin J. – POW*
Doel, Trooper Lloyd G. – POW
Gill, Corporal James E. – Evaded capture until 29 October
Gold, Gunner John R. 'Ian' – POW
Haddow, Private Robin G. – POW
Hill, Trooper William R. (Ron) – POW
Knowles, Trooper George S. D. – POW
Magee, Trooper J. B. (Jack) – POW
Mallett, Trooper Hector L. – Died of wounds
McDonald, Gunner Douglas O. 'Shorty' – Evaded capture until 29 October
McKay, Private Frederick R. – POW
McLelland, Private Thomas R. – Evaded capture until 29 October
McLeod, Private Roy F. – Evaded capture until 29 October
Mitford, Trooper Peter V. R. – POW
Penhall, Trooper Archibald J. – Died of wounds
Pickering, Trooper Clyde T. – POW

* New Zealander Edwin Dobson did not survive captivity. He fell ill and died in the last weeks of the war, in April 1945.

Robinson, Gunner Frank M. – POW
Rodgers, Trooper Robert K. – POW
Scott, Gunner Lyal D. – POW
Steedman, Private Bruce – POW
Sutherland, Lieutenant/Acting Captain John M. – POW

Signallers on motor launch

Morrison, Gunner W. H. (Bill) – Returned to Leros
Unknown – Returned to Leros

APPENDIX III

X2 Patrol: Clidi

25 October–16 November 1943

Bennett, Rifleman Andrew F. – Wounded, escaped
Bremner, Signalman J. E. (Jim) – Wounded/POW
Broderick, Signalman Gordon R. 'Brick' – POW
Calder Potts, Sergeant Lorenzo 'Cito' – Wounded, escaped
Coventry, Corporal Donald T. – Escaped*
Evans, Private John A. 'Skinny' – Escaped
Foley, Private Kenneth (medic attached from RAMC) – Escaped
Lemmer, Rifleman R. N. (Ron) – POW
Malan, Rifleman Peter S. S. – POW
McLeod, Rifleman Robert I. – POW
Oelofse, Rifleman Louis J. N. – Killed on 12 November 1943
Olivey, Captain John R. – POW and later escaped
Rundle, Rifleman R. O. 'Mick' – POW
Rupping, Gunner Jacobus F. 'Jack' – Escaped
Todman, Signalman Harold A. 'Toddy' – Died of wounds
Van Rensburg, Rifleman Johannes D. – Escaped†
Winter, Acting Corporal L. P. (Peter) – POW

---

* According to Don Coventry, Signalman Watson of S1 Patrol was also among those evacuated.

† Johannes van Rensburg died as the result of a shooting accident in Greece on 2 October 1944.

Attached New Zealanders thought to include:

Ellis, Trooper Eric – Escaped
McLeod, Private Donald C. – Escaped*
Munro, Lance Corporal Douglas – Escaped

* After the British defeat in the Dodecanese, Donald McLeod was withdrawn from the LRDG together with other New Zealanders and transferred to his homeland's armed forces. He was killed while serving in Italy on 6 October 1944.

APPENDIX IV

Recommendations, Citations and Awards

Citation and award

RH/170243 Lieutenant (temporary Captain) John Richard Olivey MC
Bar to Military Cross

Capt. OLIVEY was given the task of holding a gun position in the North of LEROS and he had 11 men under his command. At the start of the battle his position was heavily attacked by infantry supported by Stukas. With his handful of men he held his ground until reinforcements arrived but later had to leave the position under extreme pressure from an enemy counter attack. Next day he personally led an attack on the position which was retaken. From then on he held the ground for the rest of the battle and his magnificent leadership and courage under many repeated attacks undoubtedly affected the course of the battle in that area. When the infantry reinforcements were withdrawn from this feature Capt. OLIVEY refused to leave and was himself still firing a Bren Gun and throwing grenades 13 hours after the Island surrendered. Throughout the battle he showed no thought for his personal safety and at times was himself firing heavy coast guns over open sights at the advancing enemy despite persistent dive bombing attacks on a very heavy scale.

Recommendation by Captain John Olivey

Signalman BREMNER remained on his set until all messages were cleared when exposed to danger from an exploding ammunition magazine.

In the battle of LEROS he remained on his set from 04.00 hours to 17.00 hours continuously passing messages – his relief having been killed. His position in the Fort was such as to expose him to continual risk. He was subsequently removed from the window – the Germans being then in possession of the entrances. His W/T set was destroyed by enemy fire whilst Signalman Bremner was endeavouring to remove it through the window. On his activities as a Signaller thus being suspended he immediately went into action with his rifle and grenades and was in the last party to leave Pt 320.

On the last day of the battle Signalman Bremner received a wound in the foot early in the morning.

It was impossible to remove him from this position until dark[.] He hobbled back however to a position from which he could report that the medical Orderly had been wounded.

Signalman Bremner showed great coolness under difficult conditions and bravery in battle.

Citation and award

RH/2552926 Signalman James E. Bremner
Military Medal

At LEROS during the assault in November 1943 Sgm BREMNER was W/T Operator to a patrol of this Unit holding a position at Mount CLIDI. He remained on his set continuously passing messages each day from 0400 to 1700 hrs despite extremely heavy attacks by ground and air forces, and continued to do so until his set was destroyed as the enemy entered the gun position where he was located. Sgm Bremner was wounded but escaped through a window to rejoin his patrol. He continued to fight and showed great courage in later assisting a wounded comrade to withdraw under heavy fire from enemy machine guns. Throughout the battle he showed very great coolness and complete disregard for danger.

Recommendation by Captain John Olivey

Before the battle of LEROS – Cpl. Coventry – whilst standing near the naval gun which received a direct hit from a bomb causing fire in the ammunition magazine showed great courage in assisting the removal of wounded and clearing the area – at the time signalling the extent of the damage and the movement of shipping to HQ.

During the battle of LEROS continually he exposed himself to danger in repulsing the enemy, assisting in the removal of the wounded and in the withdrawal from Pt 320.

Subsequently in the counter attack on Pt 320 Cpl. Coventry was largely responsible for the capture of 17 Germans who had occupied a cave on the forward slope and whose presence was holding up the advance. Cpl. Coventry with two other men moved across the enemy fire to the cave.

During the last stage of the battle Cpl. Coventry with his section held the forward slope for 24 hours – evacuating wounded by carrying them on his back up the hill.

He subsequently escaped from LEROS while the Island was occupied by the enemy.

Cpl. Coventry showed complete disregard for danger throughout the battle.

Citation and award

RH/6857923 Sergeant Donald Tudor Coventry
Distinguished Conduct Medal

At LEROS in November 1943 Sgt Coventry was part of a patrol of this unit holding the Mount CLIDI position. Before the battle began he showed great courage in assisting the removal of men who were wounded when a naval gun scored a direct hit. During the battle his complete personal disregard for safety was outstanding and with only two men was responsible for the capture of 17 Germans who were holding up our successful attempt to recapture the position. During the last phase of the battle he held the forward slopes of this feature with a handful of men until finally he ordered his party to leave while he carried 2 wounded men to safety on his back. He subsequently escaped from LEROS after the occupation by the Germans.

Recommendation by Captain John Olivey

Artillery Second Lieutenant Ferruccio Pizzigoni
Citation

At the approach of enemy shipping from the North East on [date missing] Nov. 1943 2nd Lieut Petsigonne [sic] showed considerable skill – having taken over command of the Marine battery on Pt 320. His guns being responsible for the sinking of at least two of the enemy landing craft before they could reach the island.

During the approach of the enemy to PV [sic: Pt] 320 he personally – with the assistance of one marine maintained and fired his one remaining gun – successfully repulsing attempts to land barges in the North of Leros.

When his ammunition in the local (No 2. Gun) magazine was exhausted he personally – under enemy machine gun fire – carried shells from the main magazine until assisted by British troops.

On the near approach of the enemy he organised the carrying forward of the Seotti Fascisti [sic] gun so that this could bring fire on the approaching enemy. This gun immediately became the target for mortar and rifle fire but he continued to fire until the gun was wrecked by the enemy.

2nd Lieut. Petsigonne then taking with him an Italian machine gun and ammunition advanced to the cave to the West. His gun was heard in action up to 14.00 hours when his position was overrun and captured by the enemy.

No remains of 2nd Lieut Petsigonne being found in the cave when the position was retaken – it is concluded that he was captured.

Throughout the battle 2nd Lieut Petsigonne had shown great courage and complete disregard of danger.

I have the honour to recommend 2nd Lieut Petsigonne for conspicuous skill and bravery in the face of the enemy on Point 320 Leros on the 10th [sic] November 1943.

The British chose not to formally recognise the courage shown by Pizzigoni. He was, however, honoured by his own countrymen in 1954 with the award of Italy's highest wartime decoration for bravery. A piazza in Credaro, Italy, also bears his name.

Citation and award

Medaglia d'oro al valore militare
Sottotenente d'artiglieria
Ferruccio Pizzigoni

(Translation)
Gold Medal for Military Valour
Artillery Second Lieutenant
Ferruccio Pizzigoni

As a subordinate officer at a coastal battery on an overseas island under siege by superior German forces, he positioned a machine gun on the remains of a destroyed battery gun and personally conducted highly effective fire against attacking dive-bombing aircraft. When enemy forces landed, he disregarded mortar fire and continuous low-level and dive-bombing air attacks, and commenced a relentless firing of the guns, achieving two hits and forcing enemy ships and landing craft to withdraw. Despite being wounded and with only one surviving sailor among the decimated armaments, he continued firing with two guns, loading and aiming a gun himself until reinforcements arrived, and with his remaining energy tended the wounded. Falling exhausted he revived after a short pause and resumed the fierce struggle undaunted, until the heroic garrison was overwhelmed after long hours of combat, whereupon he destroyed the remaining serviceable guns. Captured by the enemy, fully aware of the brutal reprisals and despite having the opportunity to escape by remaining among the ranks of ordinary soldiers, he revealed his then-unapparent officer status to share the fate of his comrades. Slain, he fell, demonstrating by his ultimate sacrifice remarkable military virtues and sublime dedication to duty.

(Leros 12.11.1943)

Citation and award

Medaglia d'argento al valore militare
Tenente di artiglieria compl.
Daniele Pieri

(Translation)
Silver Medal for Military Valour
Artillery Lieutenant
Daniele Pieri

Commander of anti-ship battery at an overseas naval base – subjected to violent enemy siege – courageously and skilfully directed defensive fire to counter mortar fire and intense enemy air attacks. He repeatedly hit landing craft and succeeded in repelling enemy units providing support from offshore. Attacked from land and sea, after fourteen hours of heroic resistance, with decimated personnel, and unable to continue firing, he blew up the battery. He was captured by the enemy and killed, demonstrating to the end his high military virtues.

(Leros, 8 September–12 November 1943)

The award was made in 1952. Daniele Pieri was further honoured with having a piazza named after him in his municipality, San Romano in Garfagnana.

APPENDIX V

Glossary

2 i/c	Second-in-command
2/Lt	Second lieutenant
A/A	Anti-aircraft
BYMS	British Yard Minesweeper
CO, C.O.	Commanding officer
CP	Command post
H.E.	High explosive
HM	His Majesty
H.M.L.S.	His Majesty's Levant Schooner (usually abbreviated L.S.)
HMS	His Majesty's Ship
HMS/M	His Majesty's Submarine
HQ, H.Q.	Headquarters
I.O.	Intelligence officer
LRDG, L.R.D.G.	Long Range Desert Group
LSF	Levant Schooner Flotilla
MC, M.C.	Military Cross
ME, M.E.	Middle East
MFP	*Marinefährprahme* (Ger. F-lighter/type of landing craft)
M.G.	Machine gun
M.I.(9, etc.)	Military Intelligence (section 9, etc.)
ML, M.L.	Motor Launch
MTB	Motor Torpedo Boat
N.C.O.	Non-commissioned officer
NZ	New Zealander
OC, O.C.	Officer commanding

OP, O.P.	Observation Post
OR	Other rank (non-commissioned)
POW, P.O.W.	Prisoner of war
Q, Q.	Quartermaster
RAF, R.A.F.	Royal Air Force
R.F.	Raiding Forces
RV, R.V.	Rendezvous
SAS, S.A.S.	Special Air Service
SBS	Special Boat Squadron
SIME	Security Intelligence Middle East
TSMG	Thompson sub-machine gun
UJ	*Unterseebootjäger* (Ger. submarine-attack craft)
W/T	Wireless telegraphy (radio)

APPENDIX VI

German Land Forces

I./Fallschirmjäger-Rgt.2
I. Bataillon/Fallschirmjägerregiment 2
II./Gren.Rgt.16
II. Bataillon/Grenadierregiment 16
II./Gren.Rgt.65
II. Bataillon/Grenadierregiment 65
5./Gren.Rgt.65
5. Kompanie/II. Bataillon/Grenadierregiment 65
II./Lw.-Jg.Rgt.22
II. Bataillon/Luftwaffen-Jägerregiment 22
6./Lw.-Jg.Rgt.22
6. Kompanie/II. Bataillon/Luftwaffen-Jägerregiment 22
7./Lw.-Jg.Rgt.22
7. Kompanie/II. Bataillon/Luftwaffen-Jägerregiment 22
8./Lw.-Jg.Rgt.22
8. Kompanie/II. Bataillon/Luftwaffen-Jägerregiment 22
III./Gren.Rgt.440
III. Bataillon/Grenadierregiment 440
1./1.Rgt. 'Brandenburg'
1. Kompanie/1. Regiment 'Brandenburg'
1./Küstenjäger-Abt. 'Brandenburg'
1. Kompanie/Küstenjäger-Abteilung 'Brandenburg'
15./4.Rgt. 'Brandenburg'
15. Kompanie (Fallschirmjäger)/4. Regiment 'Brandenburg'
11./Lw.-Jg.Rgt.21
11. Kompanie/III. Bataillon/Luftwaffen-Jägerregiment 21

Further Reading

Nearly all books about the Long Range Desert Group focus on the war in North Africa. What little there is about the role of the LRDG in the Aegean and elsewhere is usually to be found in books with a broader theme.

Crichton-Stuart, Michael, *G Patrol: The Story of the Guards Patrol of the Long Range Desert Group* (William Kimber and Co., 1958).

Gross, Kuno, with Roberto Chiarvetto and Brendan O'Carroll, *Incident at Jebel Sherif: In Search of the First Clash of the Special Forces 1941/2009* (Kuno Gross, 2009).

Kay, R. L., *Long Range Desert Group in the Mediterranean* (War History Branch, Department of Internal Affairs, Wellington, New Zealand, 1950).

Kennedy Shaw, W. B., *Long Range Desert Group: The Story of Its Work in Libya, 1940–1943* (Collins, 1945).

Lloyd Owen, Lt.-Col. David, DSO, OBE, MC, *The Desert My Dwelling Place: With the Long Range Desert Group in North Africa* (Cassell and Co., 1957).

Lloyd Owen, Major-General David L., CB, DSO, OBE, MC, *Providence their Guide: The Long Range Desert Group 1940–45* (George G. Harrap & Co., 1980).

Morgan, Mike, *Sting of the Scorpion: The Inside Story of the Long Range Desert Group* (Sutton Publishing, 2000).

Mortimer, Gavin, *The Men Who Made the SAS: The History of the Long Range Desert Group* (Constable, 2015).

O'Carroll, Brendan, *Fighting with the Long Range Desert Group: Merlyn Craw MM's War 1940–1945* (Pen & Sword Military, 2022).

O'Carroll, Brendan, *The Kiwi Scorpions: The Story of the New Zealanders in the Long Range Desert Group* (Token Publishing, 2000).

O'Carroll, Brendan, *The Long Range Desert Group in Action 1940–1943* (Pen & Sword Military, 2020).

O'Carroll, Brendan, *The Long Range Desert Group in the Aegean* (Pen & Sword Military, 2020).

O'Carroll, Brendan, *R Patrol Long Range Desert Group* (Pen & Sword Military, 2024).

Pittaway, Jonathan, *Long Range Desert Group, Rhodesia: The Men Speak*, (agencies@iafrica.com, undated).

Pittaway, Jonathan and Craig Fourie, *LRDG Rhodesia: Rhodesians in the Long Range Desert Group* (Dandy Agencies, 2020).

Rogers, Anthony, *Churchill's Folly: Leros and the Aegean, The Last Great British Defeat of World War Two* (Cassell, 2003).

Rogers, Anthony, *Kos and Leros 1943: The German Conquest of the Dodecanese* (Osprey Publishing, 2019).

Rogers, Anthony, *Swastika over the Aegean: September–November 1943*, (toro.enquiries@gmail.com, 2013).

Thompson, Julian, *War Behind Enemy Lines* (Sidgwick & Jackson, 1998).

X, Ex-Lance-Corporal, QGM, *The SAS and LRDG Roll of Honour 1941–47* (SAS-LRDG-RoH, 2016).

Periodicals

Gross, Kuno, *Tracks: The Magazine commemorating the Long Range Desert Group* (info@desertstories.org, published yearly).

Index

Page numbers in italics refer to appendices and notes.